what I know about

BASEBALL

is what I know about

LIFE

what I know about BASEBALL is what I know about LIFE

Peter G. Doumit

Tate Publishing & *Enterprises*

TATE PUBLISHING
& Enterprises

Tate Publishing is committed to excellence in the publishing industry. Our staff of highly trained professionals, including editors, graphic designers, and marketing personnel, work together to produce the very finest books available. The company reflects the philosophy established by the founders, based on Psalms 68:11,

"THE LORD GAVE THE WORD AND GREAT WAS THE COMPANY OF THOSE WHO PUBLISHED IT."

If you would like further information, please contact us:
1.888.361.9473 | www.tatepublishing.com
TATE PUBLISHING *& Enterprises*, LLC | 127 E. Trade Center Terrace
Mustang, Oklahoma 73064 USA

What I Know about Baseball is What I Know about Life

This title is also available as a Tate Out Loud product.

Cover design by Janae J. Glass
Interior design by Chris Webb

Published in the United States of America

ISBN: 978-1-6024716-4-1

09.05.14

Dedication

To my wife, Faith, for her unconditional support and encouragement;

to my children, Patrick, Amy, Peter and Ryan for being some of my greatest teachers;

to my parents and brothers and sisters for molding me into the person I am;

to my students and athletes over my career who gave me a chance to do what I felt called to do—teach and coach;

and finally, to the Good Lord, from whom all good blessings come and for whom I wish to serve.

Acknowledgements

All books reflect, to varying degrees, the author's background, personality, insights and opinions about not only the topic material, but often their life view as well. This book is no exception and I am indebted to many people who have influenced me along the way.

First and foremost are my parents, Eli and Patricia Doumit, who raised my ten brothers and sisters and me in a household where faith, hope and love were abundant, and hard work, discipline and respect were expected. They were my first teachers and models and I have attempted to live the type of life befitting of their upbringing.

My brothers and sisters were very instrumental in my life's lessons as well. Being the second oldest of eleven provided opportunities–both wanted and unwanted–that nevertheless added to my store of experiences providing a framework for developing my philosophy regarding relationships with others, teamwork, loyalty and perseverance.

I have been strongly influenced as a teacher and coach throughout my career by five premiere coaches who I have attempted to emulate in as much as my personality would allow. Chuck "Bobo" Brayton, my baseball coach at Washington State University, was instrumental in giving me a thorough knowledge of the game as well as giving me a chance to be part of a program as a player and coach that I longed to be part of. Over the years he has continued to be a friend and mentor and I will always be indebted to him for seeing something in me that could be developed.

Ad Rutschman, retired baseball coach and athletic director at Linfield College, continued my education as a baseball coach and molder of young people when I was fortunate enough to be a graduate assistant in his highly successful program. Ad was a tremendous mentor in the art of teambuilding and relationship building in addition to being an extremely knowledgeable coach.

Ed Cheff, the highly successful baseball coach at Lewis-Clark State College in Idaho is, in my estimation, the most technically knowledgeable coach I have ever encountered. There is no part of the game–even in its smallest detail–that Ed has not analyzed and coached. He leaves no stone unturned and his analysis and instruction are based on solid reason. His results bespeak his process. I am indebted to him for his willingness to share his knowledge and philosophies which I have borrowed from extensively.

The current baseball coach at Linfield College, Scott Carnahan, is another man from whom I have learned and incorporated much. Scott and I are close in age and I relished the time when we were both young coaches and I was able to be an assistant in his first college coaching position. Scott is a great communicator with exceptional knowledge of both people and baseball and I have appreciated his insights and encouragement throughout the years.

The last coach, that perhaps has had the greatest impact on me, is a man whom I've never met personally, though I did share correspondence with him once. John Wooden, legendary basketball teacher (as he would prefer to be known), has had more influence on my teaching and coaching philosophy than perhaps anyone other than my parents (and Coach Wooden's philosophy and my parents' philosophy are grounded in the same moral principles and Christian tenets). Coach Wooden's emphasis on the process rather than the outcome and building good people as well as good athletes became the main focuses in my coaching as well. It will hardly be a surprise, then, as one reads this book how often Coach Wooden is quoted or referred to.

To all my assistant coaches and head coaches who I've had the pleasure to work with and learn from over the years in baseball and basketball, my thanks to you all. Special thanks to my brother John, also a baseball coach and someone who shared a passion for the game when we were growing up, Rick and Kathy Koba, Mike Price, Xavier Ramos, Robert Haensel, Quintz Whitaker, Ted Wilson, Ed McNamara, Dave Johnson, Dan White, Jim Hannah, Jerry Thaut, Len Robison, Frank Rightmire, Aaron King, Roger Taylor, Dennis Davidson, Mel Louk, Mike Gomez, Aaron McLean, my son Pat Doumit and all the others who, in some way, have made an impact in my life as a teacher and coach.

To all the players–from t-ball to semi-pro; male and female; in baseball and basketball; in all the schools and communities where I've been–thanks to you for allowing me to learn about sports and life with you.

Special thanks to Dr. Ken Ung and his wife Carol, for providing many of the pictures used in this book as well as capturing memories for us of Ryan's playing days in Pittsburgh and sharing them with us since that first season.

To the fine people at Tate Publishing who believed in my manuscript and message and have worked hard to make this dream a reality. Special thanks to Janey Hayes, the first at Tate to read and recommend my manuscript, Curtis Winkle, my editor, who helped to make it more presentable, and Janae Glass, who did a terrific job with the cover design.

Finally, to my wife Faith and my extended family for the love and support over the lean years as well as the good ones. I couldn't have done it without you.

Table of Contents

Foreword

The teachings of my father have unquestionably laid the foundation of my baseball education. Many of the findings in this book have paved the groundwork for where I am today as a player.

Working my way through the minor leagues, rarely was there a situation or technique new to me in the sense of me not hearing it before in some shape or form. Now, as a major leaguer, on the biggest stage where everything is under the microscope, I still look to my father for knowledge and inspiration.

I have had the opportunity to work with some of the best coaches and instructors in the world, many of them for which I have the utmost admiration and respect, but I have been truly blessed to have my greatest coach also be my father.

—Ryan Doumit
Pittsburgh Pirates

Introduction

When I sat down to actually begin writing this book, I bent one of the very rules that I write about in the book—the importance of beginning something with the end in mind. I had a desire to write down some of my thoughts and experiences as they relate to two important topics to me—baseball and life and the teaching about both—but I wasn't sure exactly what the "end' would be.

I am a teacher and coach, and when asked, "What do you teach and coach?" my answer is "People." I teach people, and I use baseball, life experiences and the subject matter I instruct as the medium, rather than making them the message themselves.

This is an important distinction to me. I've always tried to make the focus on my students and athletes rather than on the game or subject matter I was using to instruct them. Sports and social studies were tools to reach a greater end: to prepare my students/athletes to do well in living their lives. I want them to be thinking, productive, useful people who enjoy living and appreciate what life has to offer. To do this, I believe there are a few key concepts that can be taught by me and learned by them to help with the process.

What I Know about Baseball Is What I Know about Life is a compendium of not-so-random thoughts that are connected to carry out this mission. It is not—nor is it intended to be—a definitive work, but rather a sampling of life lessons, and baseball lessons that touch on some of the important and useful concepts employed by "successful" people as defined above.

Throughout the book there are references to developing the total person in five areas or dimensions—physical, intellectual, emotional, social and spiritual. Balance of these areas is a main theme. Religious or spiritual references are not meant to proselytize but to try to explain how and why I feel this dimension is as interconnected and important in the total scheme of things as the other dimensions. The readers are left to discern how they will deal with this dimension on their own. References that I make are used as examples of how this dimension has been applied by me in dealing with the often complex and confusing thing sometimes referred to as "the game of life."

It is my wish that the reader finds, within the book, food for thought, inspiration, a growth in perspective, perhaps a little humor, a greater understanding of the game of baseball and its connection to life, and most importantly, a reason for hope—for the future, for humankind, for living life as fully as it can be lived. I send you forth with the words of John Calvin, "The word hope I take for faith; and indeed hope is nothing else but the constancy of faith."

> "Get a good pitch to hit, keep your eyes on the ball,
> and swing hard in case you hit it! Now, Play Ball!"

—Pete Doumit
March 2007

"Keep Your Eyes On The Ball."

—Baseball's/Life's First Lesson
From Father to Son

Baseball the Metaphor . . .

Baseball—in fact every sport—is used as a metaphor for life. I believe sports were created to teach the essential lessons of life that we all need to learn in order to live a useful, productive, and yes, "successful" life.

Sports can be an instruction manual as well as practical application for dealing with the challenges of life. In all lives there will be successes and failures, errors, injuries, bad hops, tough plays, strikeouts and home runs. There will be times when the grass is green, the sun is shining and every ball we hit finds a hole. When the ball seems as big as a grapefruit, we are "in the zone" and we can do no wrong. It seems like such an easy game . . .

Then there are the times when we are in a slump, we can't buy a hit even when we seem to be doing everything right. The clouds foreboding rain are nothing compared to the clouds in our mind causing us to wonder about ourselves, our ability, why the ball looks so small when we're trying to hit it. It is such a frustrating game . . .

Contrary to what it says on the t-shirt, baseball isn't life. Nor is it—or should it be—a life or death situation. Baseball—and life—I believe, is not an easy game, but it is a simple one. The basic principles of both are simple: learn the proper fundamentals, practice them over and over to become proficient at them, play with passion and enthusiasm while always giving your best effort, be the best teammate you can be, accept with grace and humility the outcome knowing that whatever the outcome may be, success is ultimately measured by what you have done with what you have been given (talent-wise).

There is more to baseball and life than just keeping score. Statistics, so important to both, don't begin to measure the intrinsic, intangible feelings and emotions that are felt by those who pour their heart and soul, totally immersing themselves, into playing/living the way these are intended to be.

When one truly knows and understands the game of baseball and plays it the way it is meant to be played, then that person knows life and how it is meant to be lived.

Life's Averages

"... Success isn't figured by averages. Nobody will remember the times you struck out in the early innings - if you hit a home run with the bases full in the ninth."

—From the Toastmaster's Treasure Chest
Prochnow and Prochnow Jr.

Begin With the End in Mind

Rarely if ever does a person get into a car and start driving without a destination in mind. Even if this does occur, it is not long before decisions are made to turn, go straight, stop, or go on. The point is we are always going somewhere; the important thing is do we know where that somewhere is?

So much of life depends on where we choose to go. Yet so often we get a delayed start on this process. When are we old enough to understand the importance of "beginning with the end in mind"? Put another way, are little children too young to begin to dream and become the type of person they would like to become?

Beginning with the end in mind to me refers more to having a vision about the kind of person one would choose to be rather than an occupation or accomplishment that one would aspire to become or attain. Learning and inculcating universal virtues and skills such as honesty, a strong work ethic, compassion, trustworthiness, communication, respect, accountability, responsibility, humility and the like are the building blocks for one to become or achieve whatever they choose.

This notion of beginning with the end in mind is closely associated with the notion of leaving a legacy. What do you want to accomplish? What would you like to have said about you upon the end of your career, or your retirement, or in your obituary? What mark do you want to leave on this world that you will be remembered for? What difference will you have made in the world because of your life? How will you have impacted the lives of others? How will you feel about how you've spent your life?

Each new baseball season provides me as a coach an opportunity to reflect on these questions and to assist my team members with addressing them. Perhaps, for many, it is the first time that they have pondered these questions to any degree. Others, because of life experiences, may have had a head start on them. To me, it is the beginning of team building where players must first come to grips with a perception of themselves and what they want to become. The next step is for them to see how all the individual pieces can be put together to accomplish a common purpose. When this occurs, it is the greatest thrill in coaching—even better than winning a game—because each player becomes a "win" and, collectively as a team, they become "winners."

Becoming accustomed to "begin with the end in mind" is a habit applicable to all areas of our lives. It becomes a mental road map that can keep us on the path to achieving what we want to achieve, doing what we want to do, going where we want to go, and becoming what we want to become as a person. It can help us to avoid the dead ends, wrong turns or time "being lost" and wasting our precious "life fuel" of time in the process.

Knowing where we are headed and knowing how to get there makes traveling much more enjoyable and much less stressful. And it all begins when we have the end in mind.

"You've got to be careful if you don't know where
you're going 'cause you might not get there."
"If you don't set goals, you can't regret not reaching them."

—Yogi Berra
from The Yogi Book

Playing the Nine Best or the Best Nine?

Synergy—When the combined action of individual contributions is greater in total effect than the sum of its parts.

(1+1+1+1+1+1+1+1+1=>9)

Baseball, like many other sports, is a team game in the sense that on the scoreboard it pits one team against another. Nine players take the field for each team and nine players bat. Most teams have additional players—I like to refer to them as "reserves" rather than substitutes because I think the connotation is more meaningful—that can be inserted into the game whenever the coach or manager believes it will benefit the team to do so.

Baseball, to a degree, resembles individual sports like tennis, wrestling, golf, and swimming[1] also, because of the critical individual match up that takes place between the pitcher and the batter. At that time it is mano y mano and no one can help you once you step into the batter's box or step on the pitcher's rubber to deliver the pitch. Situationally, you are on your own to hit, pitch, field a ball or run the bases to the best of your ability; but how well you and your teammates do this collectively determines how good a team you have.

To take this "game within a game" (individual competition within a team framework) a step further, there are other "competitions" at play. The catcher and pitcher form a two against one team to try to get the hitter out. The catcher suggests a type of pitch and a location for it; it's up to the pitcher to throw a good pitch. (Any pitch, perhaps, that gets a hitter out is considered a "good" pitch regardless if it was thrown where and the way the pitcher/catcher wanted it to be.) If the batter hits the ball, now the game becomes a team game. An individual must catch it, and oftentimes, is required to throw it to another teammate to retire the batter or get him out. Again, the more consistently individuals can work together to perform these skills, the better the team will be.

So, it would stand to reason that if a coach were to put the nine best individual players out on the field, that team would have the best chance to win. Right?

That was a trick question. The answer is: not always. First of all, the best team doesn't always win. As discussed elsewhere, there are too many variables in baseball to be able to say with absolute certainty that the squad with the best individual players will always win. From personal experience, take my word for it, it just doesn't happen.

Secondly, again through personal experience as both a player and coach, I have discovered that there is quite a difference between fielding the best nine players and the nine best players.

I first heard this distinction in terminology from my college baseball coach, Bobo Brayton, at Washington State University back in the early 1970's. He told us that he was committed to putting the "best nine," that is the best *team* of players in his judgment—players who worked cohesively as a unit; selfless players who would sacrifice individual glory for the good of the team—on the field for each game. This "best nine," he explained, might not be the nine most talented players he had. He distinguished between a collection of talented individuals who can play (nine best) and a *team* of players who, when playing together, transformed into something greater than the collective talents of the individuals. (In other words, a synergetic body, or what I would say is the best definition for *team*.)

Now, I don't ever recall Coach Brayton referring to this phenomenon as synergy. In fact, I don't believe I ever even heard the word until the mid 1980's, and I'm not so sure Coach even knew the name for it. But I do remember the concept even though, at the time, it didn't have a name other than "teamwork."

Great talent is a gift, but it is a compounded gift when one is able to mesh it with other talent in an unselfish way to transform it into something truly special. I believe that talent is not "ours" per se, but something that has been given to us—perhaps loaned to us?—for the purpose of investing to reap the greatest returns. This only happens when we share it with others in combination with their gifts to do all that we can do, and become all that we can become, as individual "players" as well as true members of the human "team."

I've always tried to follow my coach's example to develop, then field, the "best nine."

The "Best Nine" Elements of a Successful Team
"Champions Field"

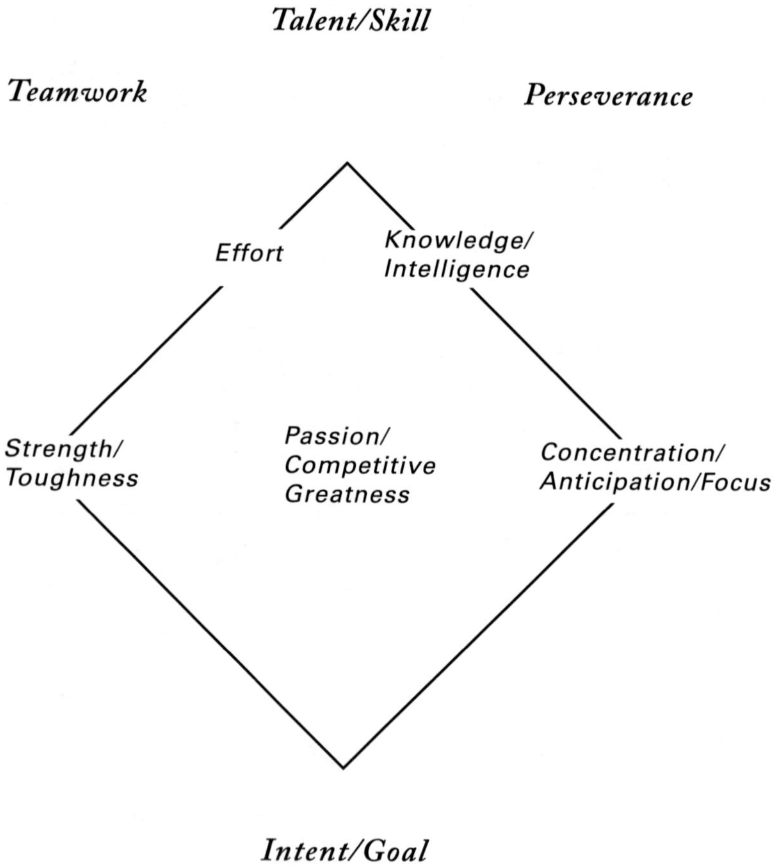

The concept of the "Best Nine" got me to thinking about putting together some kind of a visual aid for my players, using a diagram of the baseball diamond and positions to explain to them what I felt were the most important elements or qualities that it takes to be a quality baseball team. Though there are more than nine elements per se, I have arranged them into the nine positions on the baseball field.

As one may have guessed, I have been greatly influenced in my teaching and coaching by John Wooden, legendary basketball coach at UCLA, whose use of his famous Pyramid of Success was my inspiration for drawing my "Champions Field."

Following is a brief description of each element and why it was placed specifically where it is on the diagram.

Intent/Goal—Home Plate

All journeys have a beginning and end—an alpha and omega. Journeys begin with a goal in mind and the intentness to see the journey through. Without a goal and the intentness to carry it out, life can be an aimless venture. Baseball's adventure begins at home plate, follows a designed path, and, if all goes well (for the offensive team), ends back home with a run scoring—a successful journey completed. The guardian of the plate, the catcher, has an equally important goal and intent as the batter's adversary. Success often goes to the one who, perhaps, is stronger in his mission.

Passion/Competitive Greatness—*Pitcher's Mound*

It has been said that pitching accounts for up to 70–80% of a team's success. Good pitching beats good hitting usually at about that same rate. Pitchers, then, are looked to for their leadership. Nothing happens in baseball until the pitcher throws the ball. Therefore, a team needs its leader to have great passion and to demonstrate competitive greatness. Coach Wooden defined competitive greatness as, "Being at your best when your best is needed. Enjoyment of a difficult challenge." That pretty much says it all.

Concentration/Anticipation/Focus—*First Base*

These three closely connected characteristics are elements essential for consistent, quality play. Every great individual player and every great team has developed them to a high degree. Next to the pitcher and catcher, the first baseman is probably the busiest player on the field. This position requires these three elements in abundance and no team is successful without them.

Knowledge/Intelligence—*Second Base*

One of the great truths about building a strong baseball team is that the team must be strong "up the middle." i.e. your best defensive players must be in the positions in the center of the diamond—catcher, pitcher, second baseman, shortstop, and center fielder.

The same holds true with developing the "Champions Field." The elements up the middle are perhaps the most essential, though not necessarily more important, than the others in order to be successful. Knowledge and intelligence—knowing how the game is played and playing it with understanding—are key elements of being strong "up the middle."

Effort—*Shortstop*

Perhaps a team's greatest athlete is found at shortstop because of the "tools" i.e. quickness, strong arm, soft hands, range, consistency, etc. required to play there. Effort is to the Championship Field what the required tools are to the shortstop. A team simply can not be all it can be without great effort—or a quality shortstop!

Strength/Toughness—*Third Base*

Third base is referred to as the "hot corner" because of its close proximity to the right handed batter's box. Most hitters in baseball are right handed, and when the ball is pulled with power down the left field line, it can get to the third base area very quickly. A third baseman must have the qualities of toughness, agility and strength in order to survive at that position. It is not a position for the timid or weak at heart. Also, corner positions on the diamond—first and third base, and left and right field—are deemed to be "power" positions offensively. These players are expected not only to be good defenders, but also the ones most responsible for hitting the ball for power and driving in runs.

Teamwork—*Left Field*

As mentioned above, as a corner position, left field is considered a power position. Often, this position is where teams may put their weakest defender but, because of the offensive potential the player brings, they have to find a place for him to play. This is not the intent on the Champions Field. Every element or quality is an "all-star" for both offensive and defensive abilities; in other words, it is essential to the total team makeup. No pitcher is willing to go to the mound and pitch without his whole team—including his left fielder—out there behind him.

Talent/Skill—*Center Field*

As mentioned earlier, a team must be strong up the middle. Nobody—regardless of how good a coach they are—can win without having talented players with honed skills. These qualities are essential. However, there are many people who have great talent or skill that don't amount to much because these weren't channeled or developed to their fullest extent. The center fielder is considered the captain of the outfield and must be willing and capable of taking charge and providing leadership for the others.

Perseverance—*Right Field*

Right field is often the position, especially in the youth phase of development, where the weakest player is sent to play. If those players stick it out and continue to develop as players, they demonstrate this quality on the Champions Field exceptionally well. Baseball requires perseverance in order to succeed. This quality develops into a "power position" because of its importance to the overall success of an individual or team. In major league baseball the right fielder has the strongest arm of all the fielders. Without perseverance, a team would be without one of its most important pieces.

"Now this is the Law of the Jungle–
As old and as true as the sky,
And the Wolf that shall keep it
will prosper, but the Wolf that
shall break it must die.
As the creeper that girdles the
tree-trunk the Law runneth
forward and back–
For the strength of the Pack is
the Wolf, and the strength of the
Wolf is the Pack."

—Rudyard Kipling
from The Jungle Book

All Success Doesn't Look the Same . . .

"Success is a different thing to every man."
—William Feather

What is *success*?

Depending on the goal, measurement standards, situation and circumstances and many other factors, there could be as many definitions for success as there are opportunities to do anything.

Webster's New World Dictionary lends us this as its first definition: "*a favorable result.*" Again, what is favorable may be in the eye of the beholder in regard to the conditions mentioned above. What were the goals and expectations? What measures were used to determine this favorable result? Were there extenuating factors in the circumstances being judged? Was the success being measured against someone/thing else or was it being measured against its own personal best? Is intrinsic success (often the immeasurable kind which would include effort, desire, hustle, loyalty, integrity, etc.) as important as the measurable, statistical success?

Baseball is a game of numbers. There seems to be a statistic for everything and for all aspects of the game. It is so easy to fall into the habit of making comparisons between players based upon their batting averages or earned run averages, won/lost record, percentages for this or that. And these comparisons, to a degree, are helpful, interesting and legitimate in determining who is a "good, better or the best" baseball player . . . but not always. Statistics just don't—can't—measure everything. And, as any mathematician can tell you, depending on whose using them, numbers can be used to support almost anything.

As a teacher, I often ask my students what their definition of success is. Not surprisingly, the large majority of high school teens equate success with material wealth, fame, possessions, and status. They define success for themselves as having lots of money, a nice house, fancy car, prestigious occupation, lots of friends and "toys." Some make the assumption that, having grown up in this situation, it is only natural for them to think that they will continue to live this lifestyle. Others, who haven't necessarily grown up this way, equate gaining these things as a sure measure of success or failure.

What I try to help them understand is that what they are—not what they have, attain or obtain—is perhaps a greater measure of success.

> "What we are is God's gift to us. What we become is our gift to God." - Eleanor Powell

I maintain that earning the respect, first from themselves, then from those who matter to them, i.e. their teammates, family members, friends, etc. is a greater, more fulfilling definition of success. They know the characteristics they respect in others; those are what I encourage them to develop within themselves. I refer to this as "passing the mirror test." If they have developed the characteristics within themselves that they respect in others, they should like who they see in the mirror.

As mentioned elsewhere in this book, baseball is, by and

large, a game of failure. When a hitter who fails 70% of the time is considered an outstanding hitter, it illustrates the point that success doesn't always look the same. Can you imagine how long a field goal kicker in the NFL would last if he only made 30% of his field goals? Or an NBA player who only consistently made 30% of his shots? Or how about a doctor or lawyer who only had a 30% success rate in their occupations?

John Wooden's definition of success, to me, is the one that comes closest to what I try to live by and share with my own family, students and athletes:

> "Success is peace of mind that is a direct result of self-satisfaction in knowing that you made the effort to become the best you are capable of becoming."

By applying this definition, it provides a healthy perspective on what winning and success are as well as helping to keep in perspective our next topic . . . That all losses don't mean failure.

. . . And All Losses Aren't Failures, Nor Failures Losses

"There are no failures—just disappointments—
when you have done your best."
—John Wooden

Just as all success doesn't look the same, so it is that all losses aren't failures, nor failures losses. Again, this goes back to one's definition of success, but I find it truly hard to tell someone that s/he is a failure when one has done her/his best at something.

Who can ask more of a man
Than giving all within his span?
Giving all, it seems to me,
Is not so far from victory.
—George Moriarty,
'The Road Ahead of the Road Behind'

If your bottom line is only the won/loss column without regard to ability, effort, task, expectations, circumstances and the like, then success and failure is a black and white situation. But I have learned in over 30 years in teaching and coaching and

50+ years of living that life has a whole lot of grey areas in it. There are many things that can alter one's perspective of wins and losses, especially when dealing with kids and baseball.

Let me give you a couple of examples of this, but before I do, let me share a working definition for the word failure. If success was, as Wooden suggested, "making the effort to become the best that one was capable of becoming," then failure can be defined as simply not trying or not making one's best effort at any endeavor with which one is involved.

As a young man, I had just taken over the head coaching position at the second high school at which I had taught. I was replacing a very good, young and popular coach who had taken a position elsewhere. My team was a talented, senior-laden team with high expectations to win the first league championship in over twenty-five years for the school.

The season came down to the final scheduled doubleheader with our team one game behind in the standings to the team we were scheduled to play. We needed to sweep our opponent in order to win the championship and earn a berth to the state championship tournament.

At practice the day before the final games, I had a meeting with our players to explain my expectations for the day's practice and to set the tone for a focused and meaningful practice. I was coaching alone and had to rely on our players to be self-monitoring when doing things without direct supervision from me. Under the circumstances, with the importance of the next day's games and the fact that this was a team predominately comprised of seniors, I was more than a little upset when, during the course of practice, two of our best players—one senior and one junior (and leaders!)—were fooling around at the far side of the field, throwing their gloves at each other and chasing each other while some of their teammates stood around and watched. (I was throwing batting practice to half of the team on the main diamond while the other half was at another cage for hitting practice.)

I chastised them (and the others) for making a mockery of practice, sent them home and subsequently announced before the game that I would not start them (after much soul-searching and a restless night) in the first game the next day.

I had a mutiny on my hands. With the game ready to start, my team sat in the dugout and informed me that if the two "stars" (both were all-conference players the year before) didn't play, they weren't going to play. Furthermore, if I didn't allow them to play, I was taking away their chance to win the league championship—I wasn't being fair.

This was one of the most difficult dilemmas I have had to deal with in my teaching/coaching career and was to become a foundation for whatever success I may have had in subsequent years in both the classroom and athletic arenas.

I told my boys that I was prepared to forfeit the games if I needed to, but as long as we had enough players who were willing to play hard I believed we still had a chance to win. I further stated that it wasn't I who had been unfair to them but their two teammates who had breached the team's covenant. It was my job to enforce team rules and expectations fairly regardless of who violated them.

Begrudgingly, the game was begun and remained a scoreless tie for four innings at which time I inserted the two disciplined players. As Providence would have it, a ball was hit toward one of the newly inserted players in the outfield who attempted to make a great catch but was unsuccessful. The ball got by him for a triple. The runner scored later in the inning accounting for the only run of the game. We were defeated 1–0 and with that defeat so went our chance for the championship.

But we still had to play the second game and, though it

couldn't make a difference in the standings, it was to be our last game as a team and the end to a bittersweet season. We ended up winning with the two boys who had been benched playing instrumental roles in the victory.

There was much dissention, hard feelings and ill-will after the game by some of the players and by some of the parents toward me. Some threatened to have my job taken from me, some of the players were confused and bewildered and disappointed that the season ended as it did.

The following year, determined to never go through another situation like that again, I prepared a contract for my players and parents to sign explaining team rules and expectations. Each contract needed to be signed and returned before a player could turn out.

One of the players from the previous year who was involved in the incident—now a senior—came up after the meeting and said that he wanted to play baseball and he knew he could play for me, but he just couldn't bring himself to sign the contract because, as he put it, I would "hold it over his head" during the season and hold the incident from the previous year against him.

Because I had had this young man in my classes that year as well and had been involved as an assistant coach with the basketball team of which he was a key player, I felt that we had grown to know and respect each other better since the previous spring. He was adamant, however, that he could not sign that contract for the reason given above.

Dilemma number two and another cornerstone of the foundation. Alone in that room, and with his solemn promise to uphold everything that was in the contract, with the penalty being removal from the team for the slightest offense, he and I shook hands on the agreement without him having to sign it. I took his word as a bond and I am happy to report that it was one of the best decisions and one of the most enjoyable seasons that both he and I ever were involved in. We won the league championship, the first baseball championship for that school in over a quarter century, and finished third in the state tournament.

After the season, this young man came to me and told me that he had never enjoyed a season in any sport (he was a three sport letterman for all four years of high school as well as an all-conference player in all three sports) more than that baseball season of 1977. I told him that to me, he was the biggest win of the season.

What is the primary goal when trying to hit a baseball? This is not meant to be a trick question, but I'm sure the answer for many is to get on base or get a base hit or to hit a home run. But I think for most baseball players and coaches—and for me—the answer is to hit the ball hard consistently.

With this in mind, consider the hitter who lines out to the shortstop, has a ball caught by the outfielder who reaches over the fence to rob him of a home run, and has another ball lined into the gap that the outfielder dives for and catches. In the scorebook he is 0–3 and his batting average is .000 for that night and his season average goes down as a result of his 0-for the night. Is he a failure as a hitter?

His statistics would suggest that, but again, most players and coaches who see this hitter may have a different perspective about him—especially if he hits the ball like that on a consistent basis.

I want that hitter to know and believe that he is a great hitter because he has done all he could do with each at bat—hit the ball hard. Once the ball leaves his bat he has absolutely no control over what is going to happen to it. Sometimes it will be caught and sometimes it will go for extra bases. All he can do is prepare to do the best he possibly can each time up, and if he can hit it hard consistently—regardless of the outcome—he is a great hitter.

Conversely, you can have a hitter who hits the ball off the handle just out of the reach of a fielder, then hits a slow roller off the end of his bat in just a place where nobody can field it in time to throw him out, then hits a pop fly to an outfielder who, at the last moment, loses it in the sun and it falls in for a base hit. This hitter is now 3–3, hitting a 1.000 for the day and his season's average has gone up.

Honestly now, with the game on the line, which of these two hitters would you want up with a chance to win the game?

The interesting thing is that in baseball, as in life most of the time, these things do tend to balance out. Over the course of the season the hitter who has hit the ball hard but right at people—what players refer to as being a victim of "at-em balls"—usually will get a close to equal number of "seeing-eye" hits, or poorly hit balls that drop in for base hits.

The point is, whether we're talking about baseball or life, one must do all within one's power—do the best one can do with what s/he has and where s/he is—and then, what happens, happens. Learn to accept it. Just as a hitter has no control over the ball once it leaves his bat, often in life we have no control over what happens to us after we have done all we can do. The key to continued success, as it has been defined here, is how well we can control our perspective about what happens to us. Again to quote the man who has had such a profound impact on me as a teacher and coach, John Wooden, "Things work out best for those who make the best out of the way things work out."

I hope these two examples illustrate how truly subjective and personal the definitions of success and failure are. Many may take issue with me on how I handled the situation with my teams back in 1976 and '77. Maybe there was a better way to handle the situation, though honestly, I would have to say that I would handle it pretty much the same way again if I found myself in the same situation.

The reason is because, from my perspective, I'm a people coach not a baseball coach. I use baseball as a means to an end. I am passionate about baseball to be sure, but only as it relates to how I can use it to build good citizens, good teammates, good people. The players are the wins that count the most.

Success for me ultimately boils down to a person utilizing the talents that s/he was blessed with to the fullest extent. Our successes and failures will ultimately be judged by the Great Score Keeper in due time. That's when our "record" will really matter.

By what measures do you want to be scored?

"Games won or lost are soon forgotten,
but the kind of person/team you are
never will be."

—Pete Doumit

Diamond Symmetry—A Lesson in Balance

Looking at a well-groomed baseball field from a position high above is a beautiful sight. The contrast of colors of the grass, dirt and chalk as well as the crispness and exactness of the lines of symmetry of the diamond produce a vision of orderliness, neatness and balance. It is no wonder that stadiums and fields have been referred to in a non-blasphemous way as cathedrals, because, in a way, they pay homage to humankind's effort to replicate the beauty and orderliness[2] of the Creator's world.

One of the greatest lessons about life that I've learned throughout my lifetime—and one that I have been constantly reminded of on the baseball diamond—is the importance of keeping all things in life in balance.

Two words—equanimity and equilibrium—best capture what I mean by balance. Both words are derived from the common Latin word aequus, which means equal or even, and are coupled with animus, meaning mind, i.e. equanimity is calmness of mind; composure; and libra, meaning balance, i.e. equilibrium is a balance between opposing forces.

Baseball is full of bad hops even when the field is well manicured. Sometimes the ball finds the little pebble or seam between dirt and grass or careens off the wall in an odd manner that causes fielders to scramble to make the play. In like manner, things pop up in our daily lives that cause an imbalance to our orderly world. Unexpected illness, receiving bad news, an embarrassing experience—these are things that can undermine our equanimity just as a contentious relationship with a coworker or a moral dilemma involving making a choice between two things of importance to you can upset one's equilibrium.

Life is a constant struggle to maintain balance. Nobody always gets perfect hops on life's playing field or gets a hit every time at bat. There will always be bad calls, bad hops and bad breaks to contend with, such as hitting the ball hard right at somebody for an out. But dealing effectively with these adversities is the very thing that creates the best, most competent and confident players. Those who learn to deal with the negatives and turbulent times of life with equanimity and equilibrium become the most competent and confident among us and can serve as models for the rest of us.

How does one learn to deal with the peaks and valleys of life with equanimity and equilibrium?

I believe that there are a number of steps in this process. First is awareness. One must be aware of the fact that all people face obstacles in life. That *is* life. And that is not a bad thing, which is the second step—perspective. It is not what happens to us that is important; it is how we respond to what happens to us that is important.

The third step is faith—faith that our loving Creator has our best interests in mind for eternity, not just for our time on earth. Faith is grasping on to the idea expressed in the passage from Romans 8:28 that there is a larger purpose than the one that we may only see from our limited perspective. A similar concept, expressed by John Wooden, famous basketball philosopher coach, is, "Things work out best for those who make the best out of the way things work out." Having the perspective and understanding that in the long run good and bad breaks tend to balance out is applying this faith.

The fourth step, and perhaps the hardest (at least for me), is trust—just letting go and letting God be in charge. Free will is ultimately making the choice to let God be in control of our lives. This doesn't mean that we become passive in our lives and reduce ourselves to merely existing or placing our lives on auto-pilot. God requires us to be active participants in all aspects of life. "Work as though everything depends on you; pray as though everything depends on God." This prayer, attributed to St. Thomas Aquinas, sums up for me what trust is all about, and the more we are able to trust, the greater we are blessed with the duel gifts of equanimity and equilibrium.

The game of baseball is comprised of two teams of equal numbers playing the same positions on the same symmetrical field with the same goal in mind. Both are facing similar obstacles but results vary due to many factors—superiority of talent of one team over the other, conditions of the playing field, momentum, and . . . the breaks of the game. The best team doesn't always win. But by maintaining balance—equanimity and equilibrium—we can enjoy all of life's travels—the journey as well as the destination.

"Man always travels along precipices. His truest obligation is to keep his balance."

—Pope John Paul II

"It's a Great Life If You Don't Weaken"

One of my dad's favorite expressions was, "It's a great life if you don't weaken."

I don't know when or where he first began saying it. I don't even know if it was an original saying from him or whether he got it from somebody else. He'd just throw it out there sometimes in the middle of a conversation, or as a summation of some point, or sometimes just as a reflection upon something he may be thinking about. I think he said it at times just to elicit a reaction or response from my siblings or me.

Now this sentiment may be trite and bordering on cliché. But, as with all clichés, there is perhaps more than just a grain of truth to it.

When life is going well, aren't we filled with boundless energy? Isn't that the time when we feel the most alive with our perceptions the sharpest and our concentration the most focused? It's a great life when we're "in the zone," when the breaks are going our way and everything couldn't be better. When this happens as a ball player, the ball looks like a beachball when you're hitting, you make defensive plays instinctively and effortlessly, and it is as if you are playing the game in slow motion. As a pitcher, you throw it where you want to when you want to with absolute command and confidence. Everything is so . . . eeeasssyyy!

Oh, to be able to formulate a potion to be able to get in the zone and stay there and stay there and stay there . . . (Maybe that's what Heaven is!)

But, just as the natural laws that say, "What goes up must come down," and "For every action there is an equal and opposite reaction," there is a flip side to being "in the zone." (Some have referred to it as "going in the toilet"!)

I'm not sure which occurs first—physical fatigue, mental fatigue or spiritual fatigue—that ushers in the sometimes gradual, sometimes precipitous descent away from "the zone" of the great life and into . . . someplace else.

In a weakened state life isn't as pleasurable. Our senses are dulled; everything becomes such an effort. Colors are not as bright; flavors aren't as full; dreams aren't as vibrant and clear. As a player it is like swinging at the ball the size of a mustard seed with a bat the width of a toothpick; the game seems to be played around you in a fast forward mode while you are in regular speed, and you understand why they refer to a fielding error as a "boot" because you kick so many of them instead of fielding them. Your pitching resembles a shotgun pattern rather than a rifle approach—it's all over the place and you have no clue where it is going once it leaves your hand. Even the simplest actions—those things you've done well a thousand times—become so . . . hhhaaarrrddd.

The worst thing that happens is the erosion of the characteristic that was so prolific in "the great life"—**hope**.

Upon reflection, that is the message that means the most to me from my dad's insight. If, somehow, we can remain hopeful through life's ebbs and flows, through its peaks and valleys, we can maintain a "great life." Maintaining equilibrium—balance—physically, mentally, spiritually, emotionally and socially is the great challenge we all face in the "game" of life. The fulcrum of this teeter-totter is hope. Without hope, life is an empty morass. With it, it's a great life.

"Take from a man his wealth, and you hinder him; take from him his purpose, and you slow him down. But take from man his hope, and you stop him. He can go on without wealth, and even without purpose, for a while. But he will not go on without hope."

—C. Neil Strait

Keeping Things in Perspective

"Everything is good or bad by comparison." That was one of my father-in-law's favorite expressions and one that I have had occasion to apply very often in my life. It is a basic truth, but one that often goes unapplied by many.

Too often we concentrate so much on how things are going from our perspective that we fail to remember or recognize that there are other perspectives, or points of view, about what's going on as well. At the moment I am writing this, our son Ryan is a major league baseball player for the Pittsburgh Pirates. He is presently in his second week of being a major leaguer and the small community that we live in has been abuzz with well-wishers and people genuinely sharing our excitement for and about him. Naturally, our hope is that he has a long and successful career filled with many highlights, few injuries and lots of fond memories along the way.

But baseball is highly competitive on many levels. There is going to be a winner and a loser; as a hitter, one has to reconcile with the fact that even great hitters fail seven out of ten times at bat. Everything seems to be measured by statistics (yet anybody who really knows baseball knows that not everything of importance is always reflected by one's stats). Then there is the constant and ferocious battle to maintain one's status on a major league roster once it has been attained. A player always knows that just as he has taken someone's spot on the 25 man roster, there are a number of aspirants attempting to do the same to him. To paraphrase Dickens, "It can be the best of times. It can be the worst of times" if one is unable to keep things in perspective.

A parent's perspective watching a ball game is quite a bit different from an ordinary fan's perspective. If the fan is rooting for the team the parents' son is playing on, they have something in common—to a degree. They both want the player to be successful; they might even share a certain passion for the success of the individual/team. But if the player isn't successful, to the fan he's a bum and they may look to some other player as the next hero; to the parent, he's still their son, and they share his frustration, disappointment and hurt when he isn't successful. (They also are immensely proud and happy when good things happen as well!)

To the fan it's "What have you done for us lately?" And often they seem to view these players as machines devoid of feelings and immune to the boos, catcalls and unkind things said to them and about them to their faces, in the press or on the television or radio. They sometimes forget that these players are people, too, with families and feelings that can be affected by what is being said.

Everything is good or bad by comparison. As I shared with my son, "Every day is a good day when you are in the major leagues. It's just that some days are better than others."

I have learned that when we compare our lives or our situations with others, there are always going to be some that are better, and there are always going to be some that are worse. Truly happy people tend to apply the wisdom of the Serenity Prayer to their lives:

> God, grant me the serenity (peace) to accept the things I cannot change . . .
> Courage to change the things I can . . .
> And Wisdom to know the difference.
> Living one day at a time,
> Enjoying one moment at a time,
> Accepting the hardships as the pathway to peace.
> Taking, as He did, this sinful world as it is, not as I would have it.
> Trusting that He will make things right if I surrender to His will.
> That I may be reasonably happy in this life,
> And supremely happy with Him forever in the next.
> Amen.
>
> (attributed to Dr. Reinhold Niebuhr)

Perspective is our view of things; how we see things and the meaning that we give to that which we perceive. We must recognize that people are going to view the same events or situations differently because of their points of view, life situations, allegiances and loyalties—and that their perceptions to them are real and true just as our perceptions, though perhaps different from theirs, are real and true. It is this difference in perspective that adds spice to life and makes for rousing rivalries. It is also a reason why there is much misunderstanding and strife in the world.

Perspective, like so many other things in life, is a double-edged sword capable of much good or much destruction depending on who is wielding it and how it is used. If we can keep in mind the basic lesson that "everything is good or bad by comparison" and recognize that there are often more perspectives than just ours—if we are able to, as is offered by the American Indian proverb, "walk a mile in another's moccasins"—then we can have greater empathy for others and expand our own perspective to truly see the "big picture" as it was intended for us to see by our Creator.

And every day that we are alive is a good day. It's just that some are better than others.

"When nothing seems to help,
I go to the stonecutter hammering away at his rock, perhaps a hundred times without as much as a crack showing in it. Yet at the hundred and first blow it will split in two, and I know it was not that blow that did it, but all that had gone before."

—Jacob Riis

Make a Difference or Make Room

Hanging on a door in my classroom is a sign that I made a number of years ago that was intended to serve as a reminder to me as to my mission as a teacher and coach:

Make a Difference or Make Room.

I have always believed—and related to my students—that they, my students, were very important and that teaching to me was more than a means of making a living. Teaching—and coaching—was a calling, a noble vocation that required able-bodied and able-minded people and demanded that those who entered into the profession be dedicated to doing the very best job possible because the stakes were so high. The stakes, of course, were the very minds of the students, and through the ripple effect, the course of our nation and, indeed, the world.

Now some may think that a rather presumptuous, bordering on egotistical, statement. That a teacher could, by him or herself, have such a far-reaching effect as to shape the minds of individuals and, in turn, affect the future of a student, citizen, community, state, nation, the world.

Can you think of a leader or prominent citizen, doctor, lawyer, engineer, businessperson—in fact any profession—that didn't have teachers? Do you suppose that those people were inspired, challenged, encouraged, maybe pushed or drug through the learning process by teachers (and coaches) as well as by their parents? Did their participation in the classroom and perhaps an athletic/activity venue help to prepare them to make the decisions they now face in their "real world" lives? Do those decisions have an effect on others?

This notion of making a difference or making room for somebody who will has been my pledge to my students and athletes as well as to myself since I began teaching over thirty years ago. It is a simple notion, but not necessarily an easy one to carry out. It is much like baseball in that the concept of the game is easy to understand. In baseball, you try to outscore your opponent by hitting the ball and running the bases within the three outs per inning that you are allotted, and try to prevent your opponent from scoring by playing catch well on defense. In teaching, you try to engage students in the development of their intellectual, physical, social, emotional (and yes, even spiritual) selves so that they can be worthwhile and productive citizens and human beings.

Often times, this is easier said than done.

Education and baseball have another thing in common—their love of statistics. Both seem to try to measure everything; all aspects are quantified first, then a "quality rating" is placed on the individual and/or performance. The one thing that neither has been able to find a way to measure with complete accuracy, however, is the size of a person's heart in respect to their desire, effort and willingness to endure virtually anything to be successful.

Both education and baseball have "naturals"—people with an abundance of talent who are capable of performing the fundamentals (of learning or of the game) effectively and efficiently.

Sometimes, however, their talent gets in the way of reaching their fullest potential because things often come too easily for them. They don't have to stretch themselves to achieve standards set or to be the best player on their team. They are able to coast while others are peddling harder to catch up or stay up with them. They often don't encounter the benefit of adversity until later in the participation process, and often are unprepared to deal with it when it inevitably comes.

This is another dimension to the "make a difference or make room" notion. Teachers and coaches must take their students where they are in their development stages in all areas—physical, intellectual, social emotional and spiritual—and attempt to move them forward. Sometimes this process is a joyous one with active, engaged students and athletes who are eager to learn and fulfill their potential . . . And sometimes it's like trying to pull teeth with them fighting you every step of the way.

I never could understand the adversarial nature of the student/teacher relationship. Why they couldn't understand that we were on their side—that we were there to help them—was always a bit of a mystery to me. It was like taking ill-tasting medicine for them; they knew it was probably good for them but that didn't mean that they had to like it! I can only deduce that it had something to do with the natural progression of maturity where defiance toward authority of any kind was a stage that all go through to varying degrees.

It says in Ecclesiastes in the Bible, "To everything there is a season . . ." This includes when it comes time for a person to take stock in what s/he is doing and how well it is being done, time for them to determine if they are still making a difference or time to make room for someone else who will be more effective.

This doesn't apply only to teachers and teaching. It can apply to all situations. And if it is time to make room it does not signal the fact that now someone is useless. It only means that it is time to move on to a new and different chapter in our life story.

"Make a difference or make room" is a challenge, an admonition, an invitation to be all we can be and do all we can do on our life's path.

This notion has served me well and it has made all the difference in the world.

"Any time you have an opportunity to make a difference in the world and you don't, then you are wasting your time on this Earth."

—Roberto Clemente

Practice Makes... Stronger Habits

The old axiom "Practice makes perfect" is arguable. There have been variables of this offered: "Perfect practice makes perfect," and "Perfect practice makes better." All have some truth to them, but do they capture the real essence of the intended thought?

Practice of any kind is primarily a matter of repetition. Anybody involved with teaching and learning (I guess that includes just about everybody!) understands the importance of repetition in learning a skill or information. Remember learning your multiplication tables? Or learning a poem or lines in a play? Or how to swing a bat or throw and field a ball correctly?

John Wooden, legendary philosopher-coach of the great UCLA basketball teams of the '60's and 70's, said this about learning in his book, *Wooden: A Lifetime of Observation and Reflections On and Off the Court* (page 144):

> The four laws of learning are explanation, demonstration, imitation, and repetition. The goal is to create a

> correct habit that can be produced instinctively under great pressure.
>
> To make sure this goal was achieved, I created eight laws of learning; namely, explanation, demonstration, imitation, repetition, repetition, repetition, and repetition.[1]

Practice—repetition—makes a habit stronger. This, of course, is a double-edged sword because habits can be good or bad. If a player is practicing how to throw incorrectly, he is probably going to become very good . . . at throwing incorrectly.

If one is taught fundamentally sound technique, then practices that technique, the results will reflect both the instruction and the repetitive practice. It all begins, then, with knowing and understanding what good fundamentals are, getting good instruction in them, then practicing them as perfectly and consistently as we can.

Perfection from imperfect beings is impossible, but it is what we, as human beings, are called to strive toward. Though unattainable, it is in the process of striving toward it that we may reach our fullest potential.

Make your strongest habits good ones!

"To give yourself the best possible chance of playing to your potential, you must prepare for every eventuality. That means practice."

– *Seve Ballesteros*

Teamwork

"Teamwork! Teamwork! That's our cry . . .
V-I-C-T-O-R-Y!
Teamwork! Teamwork! That's our plea . . .
It's our way to VIC-TOE -REE!"

That little cheer was one of the most popular cheers at the little high school I attended "back in the day" (as my students and my own children would refer to that time, long, long ago . . .). Perhaps it is one your school used, too.

Regardless of whether the little rhyme is contemporary or not, its sentiment is certainly just as applicable today as it was in yesteryear. In fact, teamwork has been in vogue since the dawn of time and is probably responsible, to some degree, for the continued existence, propagation and accomplishments of humankind.

No doubt, individuals throughout history have achieved singular fame for their inventions, innovations, thoughts and accomplishments, but . . . did they do those things completely as individuals, or did they have some kind of help along the way? Were they inspired by someone else? Did they build upon or improve somebody else's idea? Did they have any help in obtaining the education, resources and materials to achieve what they achieved?

Teamwork is the foundation for relationships. Think about it. The ultimate relationship requires love and love requires teamwork. For love to be love it must involve at least two entities with the ability to reciprocate.[3] Sharing a common goal, working together to achieve that goal, enduring the struggles and hardships together, being committed to and concerned about the welfare of each other, and ideally, sharing the success and the fruits of the labor together are all part of what it means to be a team—and to define love in a broad sense.

Following are four anagrams or sayings that have often been used when referring to teamwork that seem to capture the essence of the term for me.

There is no "I" in TEAM.

Team implies "WE" not "ME."

TEAM means *Together Everyone Achieves More.*

"People who need people are the luckiest people in the world."

Baseball is a "combination" sport. Individuals pool their talents to compete as a team for a combined outcome. One individual on the team may have a great performance day but it may not be enough to ensure victory for his team.

It can also be the case, as I know so well from being on both ends of this, that the best team doesn't always win on a given day. The great thing about a team—if it is truly a team as defined above—is that team members share the joy of winning and the agony of setbacks relationally, with each other.

I think that is what God had in mind when he created people . . . and baseball.

"Coming together is a beginning.
Keeping together is progress.
Working together
is success."

—Henry Ford

The Difference Between Knowing About and Knowing...

Oh what a chasm there is between knowing about something and truly knowing it!

A person can pick up a how-to manual on car repair, study it inside and out, take a test on it and score very well. But does that mean you would trust him to overhaul your car?

There is such a difference between knowing about something—having information about the theory, the opinions, the techniques, and on and on—and actually truly knowing something because you have experienced it. When a person has applied the knowledge, has had to adapt it to real circumstances and has used it in a real way, then, and only then, can they truly say they *know* something.

Baseball is a game with many theories. There are lots of ways to teach hitting or pitching that can lead to success. One important lesson I've learned over the 30 plus years of coaching that I have done in a variety of sports is this: *there is no such thing as a master key that will unlock all the mysteries of performing a skill for every player.* There is no one way to teach all players how to master a particular skill. Rather, there are many different ways to teach a skill that will allow a person to achieve relative success in the performance of the skill.

Good coaches (and teachers, and parents) develop a large key ring with lots of different "keys" (these come with experience!) that they can use to help the ones they are mentoring with the transition between knowing and knowing about. They will try their favorite "tried and true" method or technique that may be successful with some, many, or most of their players, but the successful ones know that they will have to use other keys to attempt to unlock both their players and the information for them.

The key here, of course, is for the coach to 1) begin with the end in mind—that is, to know exactly what he wants from his players and 2) to have enough technical knowledge to be able to teach what he wants done in a variety of ways. In other words, to have a large enough key ring with keys that will give him the greatest opportunity to unlock the mysteries of the sport for his athletes and give them the greatest chance to be successful.

The transition from knowing about to knowing occurs when the players perform with understanding the skill that has been taught. They have internalized not only the information but the application of it. When this happens, the words of the immortal Yoda of *Star Wars* fame come into play, "Do or do not—there is no try."

“Never mistake knowledge for wisdom.
One helps you make a living;
the other helps you make a life.”

—Sandra Carey

The Game of Infinite Possibilities . . .

How often, while watching or playing baseball, do you see something that you've never seen happen before? Maybe it was something quirky or bizarre; something funny or scary; something poignant or repugnant; something totally unexpected.

This, to me, is one of the great parallels between baseball and life: once you think you've seen about all there is to see, something new happens. What a blessing this is! Could you imagine how dull things would be if we'd experienced everything that could be experienced?

It is this prospect of the unknown—both in baseball and in life—that is the bait that keeps us coming back for more. It is the challenge to try one more time, to keep practicing to get just a little better; the prospect that, maybe, next time will be better, or at least different.

Regardless of what happened yesterday, or last season, hope springs eternal with new, infinite possibilities that maybe this time around it will be "our year." I think that is why baseball begins in the spring when everything is new, coming to life, fresh.

Everybody needs hope. It is life's blood. Anemic hope, weak hope, dies quickly and plunges people into an unthinkable existence. But a new hope or an enduring hope gushes and courses through people buoying their spirits and makes life worth living.

Life offers no guarantees—only a chance to play. There are no guarantees in baseball, either. There are so many variables that anything can—and often does—happen. Aren't upsets great (especially if your team is the one doing the upsetting!)? Possibilities. That's what hope offers and that is one of the greatest gifts life has to offer.

Sure, some things are predictable, routine, consistent. Those are important components of life also. They provide order out of chaos. They offer a measure of security even. But, just as all sunshine produces a desert, if everything were predictable, routine and consistent, our lives would turn from living to existing. Possibilities are what provide us with the variety that is so necessary for a full life to be lived.

Bottom of the ninth, down by one, or two, or three (it's your dream!) bases loaded, 3–2 count (or maybe you're the pitcher in this situation with the lead) . . . Ah, the possibilities! What a life!

“Become a possibilitarian. No matter how dark things seem to be or actually are, raise your sights and see possibilities—always see them, for they’re always there.”

—Norman Vincent Peale

Doumit enjoying the moment.

On deck: preparing to hit.

Hitters do their thinking "outside the box."

The essence of hitting: "See the ball; hit the ball."

Home to first: the first leg of the Tour of the Bases.

Second Base—
the "Keystone"—
Scoring position.

"Stopping at 3rd base adds nothing to the score!"

Welcome home! Victory is sweet!

Battery Power.

A diamond gem—symmetry and beauty.

The Pyramid of Participation

"Life is not a spectator sport. If you're going to spend your whole life in the grandstand just watching what goes on, in my opinion you're wasting your life."

- Jackie Robinson

As a coach it has been interesting for me to observe what I have come to refer to as the pyramid of participation in baseball. This is how it works: When children are very young, parents enroll them in a number of activities for a variety of reasons—to provide an outlet for excessive energy; to nurture some innate ability that their child may have (or the parent hopes s/he has); to encourage social and physical development; to provide the parents with perhaps a block of free time to shop, run errands, etc. while their child is under the supervision of another adult.

This ground-level swell of participation is very large and provides the base of the pyramid: lots of youngsters being introduced to the joys of the national pastime. Budding stars of all shapes and sizes (and genders) begin to learn the basics of the game—what the positions are called, which way to run on the bases, how to catch and throw, where to throw and when, how to swing a bat to make contact, and so on.

It is all uphill from there.

Some continue the ascent of the pyramid of participation the next year and in the years to follow, but many drop off along the way for a variety of reasons. Perhaps the game has never caught their imagination or they didn't find it enjoyable. Maybe they didn't see themselves as having a future past t-ball in the sport when comparing their skills—or lack thereof—with the mini-Manny Ramirezes, budding Bernie Williamses or precocious Pedro Martinezes that they were competing with. Some develop interests or passions in other areas that they have been exposed to such as a different sport or activity like music, art, or dancing. Still others give up the sport to go to work, or because they couldn't meet the expectations of others, or "just because . . ."

For whatever reason, as kids get older and as they ascend the pyramid, there are fewer players playing and they are the better players who have continued on. Only the most talented—and most dedicated, hard-working and focused—reach near the top or get to the top completely.

As a coach, I know this to be the reality of how baseball works. It is also the reality for almost any endeavor. It takes talent, dedication, encouragement, opportunity, hard work, persistence and much more to reach the top of any pyramid of participation—including life.

The qualities that are learned and developed through participation in sports and other activities—like the ones listed above—are the very same ones that serve people well in the process of participating in life.

There are many obvious similarities, I believe, between baseball's pyramid of participation and life's pyramid of participation, but there are some important differences as well.

Both progress from novice (infant) through stages of growth and competence (adolescence) until they reach the peak of their development (adult), where their fullest potential can/should be reached before aging begins to diminish skills and ability to perform at the highest levels.

Also, both are ultimately affected by life's double-edged sword known as choice. Choice is double-edged because, on the one hand, its use can lead to unhappiness, misery and unfulfilled dreams; and on the other hand, it can lead to just the opposite.

Choice is at the source of the greatest difference between the two pyramids of participation. Even though a person fails to reach his goal as a player in the game of baseball or becomes too old to effectively continue to play, he still can enjoy the game as a spectator (or coach!). There are still opportunities to cnjoy the game vicariously through the play of others.

But life, as Jackie Robinson was alluding to in his quote, is not intended to be a spectator sport. We are intended to be actively involved in the process of life with every breath that we take, including our last one.

Not every one can reach the "pro" level on the baseball pyramid, but I believe it is possible for everyone to be a "pro" in life. It is important to remember that, though pros are very good at what they do, they still make mistakes—they're not perfect. There are different levels of "pro" ball as well, from the rookie leagues to the major leagues, and even at the top level—the major leagues—people make mistakes (errors) in fielding, hitting, pitching, base running, and . . . judgment.

So to be a "pro" in life doesn't mean that we are going to be—or have to be—perfect at what we choose to do; nor does it mean that we are always going to do what we do without mistakes. The operative word here is "do." It means we are actively involved in something that we choose. It means that we are living life to the fullest rather than merely existing. It means we are in the starting lineup everyday with the opportunity to make a difference in the game. It also means that the choices we make have been well thought out so as to avoid as many errors and regrets as possible.

The ability to participate in life is the greatest gift we have. The amount of talent we are blessed with is not nearly as important as how much we use of what we are given. Full participation in life—the spending of what we have been given in a positive, useful way—can make a "pro" out of anyone who chooses to make the most of what they have.

The Baseball Pyramid of Participation

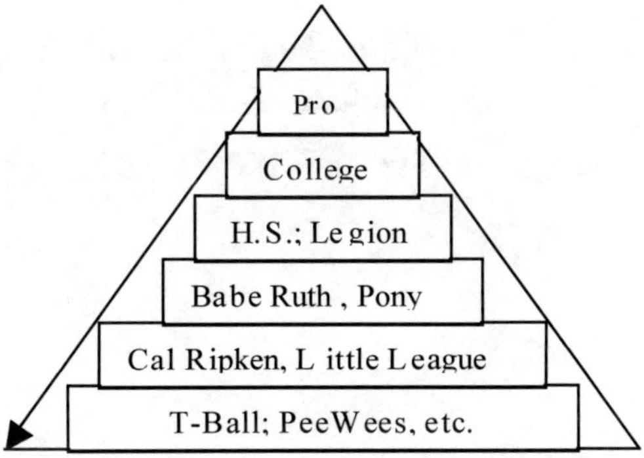

Copyright Pete Doumit 2005

With the possible exception of the foundation level, it is important to remember that each other level is stratified, i.e. at each of the above levels, exceptional performers are recognized as "all-stars" or "all-conference" or "All-Americans." Also, at the high school and college levels there are different divisions according to school size and affiliation, i.e. Division I, Division II, Division III, junior college, etc. And at the professional level there are rookie leagues, low A, high A, Double A and Triple A ball before one reaches the Major Leagues. Even at the big league level the stratification continues with all-stars from each league selected, and a World Series played between the best team from the American League and the best from the National League.

"When I stand before God at the end of my life, I would hope that I would not have a single bit of talent left, and could say, 'I used everything you gave me.'"

—Erma Louise Bombeck

The Rules of the Game

Baseball can be a harsh game. Everything may be sailing along just fine then, suddenly, everything changes. A ball takes a bad hop and the momentum of the game changes. Your team is mounting a comeback when your hitter lines into an inning-ending or game-ending double play. It can happen so quickly with no warning or notice. Regardless of the plans you've made or how prepared you have tried to be, the game—or life—throws you a curve when you're not expecting it and you are left trying to make sense of it all.

A number of years ago I was coaching a community college team and we had gotten off to a great start. Midway through the season we were 18–6 and I was envisioning a 30-win season and contemplating how deep we might be able to go in the post season. Everything and everybody was hitting on all cylinders. Every strategic move I made seemed to work and we were playing with great confidence.

Then, after a doubleheader we had just played, we were being hosted for an after-game meal at a player's parents' home. One of my better players mentioned to me that he didn't feel well; he lacked energy and just didn't seem to have the appetite to eat. I suggested that he see a doctor when we got home, and he did. The verdict: he had a full blown case of mononucleosis and was done for the rest of the season.

None of us realized that this was to signal, not only a turning point for this player, but one for our entire team. Without him in our lineup and pitching when called upon, our team lost its rhythm. We lost 13 games in a row, and only by winning the final game of the season were we able to finish 19–19 after such a promising start.

Talk about a helpless feeling! No matter what we did or how hard we tried, nothing seemed to work and no breaks seemed to come our way. After losing a number of games in a row, many of our players began to expect something bad to happen to us—and the law of the self-fulfilling prophecy seemed to be accommodating. It was one of the hardest stretches in coaching that I have ever gone through.

What this experience taught me was that there are rules regarding how the game is supposed to be played, but those rules don't determine how the ball bounces. Rules are intended to level the playing field and allow for teams to compete within guidelines equally applied to each. They are not intended to level out what happens in the course of playing the game.

It is so easy to complain about how "It's not fair!" when bad bounces or bad breaks happen in the game. The experience recounted above also taught me that life isn't fair, and that once we recognize that fact we can get along with the process of living.

Everyone throughout their lifetime is going to be a victim of bad breaks and a recipient of good breaks. Sometimes, because of our choices or our actions, these can be predictable to a degree, but most of the time life happens unscripted. In a general sense, the rule is that there are no rules when it comes to whether or not life is going to be fair. Life happens. And the ones who understand that rule won't waste precious time complaining about the fact that life isn't fair.

One of my most favorite quotes, and one that I share with my students and athletes, is by Charles Swindoll, which summarizes the biggest rule of the game:

> "The longer I live, the more I realize the impact of **attitude** on life. Attitude to me is more important than facts.... We cannot change our past... we cannot change the fact that people will act in a certain way. We cannot change the inevitable. The only thing we can do is play on the one string we have, and that is our attitude. I am convinced that life is 10 percent what happens to me and 90 percent how I react to it. And so it is with you... we are in charge of our attitudes."

Sermons We See

By Edgar Guest

I'd rather see a sermon than hear one any day;
I'd rather one should walk with me than merely tell the way.
The eye's a better pupil and more willing than the ear,
Fine counsel is confusing, but examples always clear;
And the best of all the preachers are
the men who live their creeds,
For to see good put in action is what everybody needs.
I soon can learn to do it if you'll let me see it done;
I can watch your hands in action,
but your tongue too fast may run.
And the lecture you deliver may be very wise and true,
But I'd rather get my lessons by observing what you do;
For I might misunderstand you and the high advice you give,
But there's no misunderstanding how you act and how you live.
When I see a deed of kindness, I am eager to be kind.
When a weaker brother stumbles and a strong man stays behind
Just to see if he can help him,
then the wish grows strong in me
To become as big and thoughtful as I know that friend to be.
And all travelers can witness that the best of guides today
Is not the one who tells them, but the one who shows the way.
One good man teaches many, men believe what they behold;
One deed of kindness noticed is worth forty that are told.
Who stands with men of honor learns to hold his honor dear,
For right living speaks a language which to every one is clear.
Though an able speaker charms me with his eloquence, I
say, I'd rather see a sermon than to hear one, any day.

Strategies and Gambles

Strategy, playing the percentages, calculated risks, playing a hunch, gambling—these are all a natural part of baseball . . . and life. In fact, 50% of l***if***e is ***if,*** and it comprises the core or central part of it.

Life—and baseball—offer few guarantees. Besides the old adage about the only sure things in life being death and taxes and the near certainty in baseball that the ball will find the weakest player in the most crucial time of the game, there are few certainties that apply to each.

One thing that has always fascinated me with baseball is the notion that there is a prescribed way of doing things in certain situations. This is alluded to by the expression "playing by the book." "The Book," being a book of strategy really doesn't exist except in the way the game has been taught, played and passed down through the generations as the "right way" to do things or the right strategy in certain situations to apply.

Here is an example of "book strategy." It is commonly held that when playing on the road (not in your home park where the home team would have the last chance to bat if needed) in the late innings of a close game, the visiting team would play for the winning/go ahead runs rather than to play to tie the game if that opportunity exists. In other words, say your team has a man on first in the eighth inning with no outs and you are trailing by one run. Would you consider bunting the runner to second base in this situation? You would be giving up a precious out to move the runner who only represents the tying run into scoring position with the home team always getting the last opportunity to bat. Or would you be better off going "by the book" and allowing your hitters to hit away hoping that your team can string together a few hits in a row, maybe get a break or two along the way and have a big inning?

Another example of "book strategy" that seems to be changing recently is that when a team led by five or more runs after the fifth or sixth innings, they usually would not attempt to steal bases any more because it may appear that they were "running up the score" against the opponent in an attempt to humiliate them. This notion, I have noticed, is not as prevalent these days for a couple of reasons. First, as Yogi wisely stated, "It ain't over 'til it's over." More home runs are being hit today than ever before and no lead seems safe in baseball. Rarely can a manager feel completely comfortable, even with a substantial early lead, because "it ain't over 'til it's over!" Having been in the game a long time, I have experienced both the exhilaration of a great, improbable comeback as well as the utter anguish of losing while holding a seemingly insurmountable lead.

Secondly, a reason why this strategy seems to be changing is a more "macho" approach to the game and a lessening of what was perhaps considered a more sportsmanlike approach, which was based on the Golden Rule—treat others the way you would like to be treated. Today, there seems to be a more "in your face," smack-talking indifference to how the game is played. Little consideration is shown to an opponent, and the abhorrent notion of "kicking someone while they're down" seems not so abhorrent to those who compete today. This attitude is pervasive in all areas of our society today—in business, sports, entertainment, even education—"to the winner go the spoils"—and how one achieves this is not as important as whether it is achieved.

Interestingly, just as baseball has "a book" based upon tradition and commonly held wisdom to guide it, so does life. Life's "book," the Bible—hereafter referred to as "The Book"—must have had baseball in mind from the very outset because it begins with the words, "In the big inning . . ."

Going by The Book in life offers more certainty in the outcome but is not always the easiest choice to make. Just as there are many factors involved in making a strategic decision in playing the game of baseball—including playing hunches, taking risks and gambling—there are many factors that are involved in making life choices.

People are human, fallible, often weak and don't always employ the self-discipline it takes to make the right decisions that will lead to ultimate success. We are gamblers by nature who are willing to take risks when we think we have something worthwhile or pleasurable to gain. Sometimes the risks we take are unreasonable with the possibility of losing something more valuable than what we may stand to gain. And just as some baseball managers throw away "the book" and go against what is traditional wisdom, the same happens in life with many of us.

The purpose of having "the book" in baseball and life is to provide some guidelines for how to best be successful in playing the "games." In baseball, not always going by the book can be unconventional and, because it may take our opponent by surprise, may be successful at times. The element of surprise can be an effective tool just as being unpredictable may be for a manager of a baseball team and may lead to unexpected wins occasionally.

The main differences between "the book" in baseball and The Book for life are the author and the stakes. Baseball's book is a product of man's work and is arbitrary. The Book of life is inspired by God and is definitive. For those who believe, it is not arbitrary and there will be no unexpected wins if it is followed. The ultimate win is guaranteed. Period. No ifs, ands or buts. Play by The Book and you win the greatest game of all.

And that is really the only win that counts.

"Life is an opportunity, benefit from it.
Life is beauty, admire it.
Life is bliss, taste it.
Life is a dream, realize it.
Life is a challenge, meet it.
Life is a duty, complete it.
Life is a game, play it.
Life is a promise, fulfill it.
Life is sorrow, overcome it.
Life is a song, sing it.
Life is a struggle, accept it.
Life is a tragedy, confront it.
Life is an adventure, dare it.
Life is luck, make it.
Life is too precious, do not destroy it.
Life is life, fight for it."

—*Mother Teresa*

There Is No Clock In Baseball

One of the aspects about the game of baseball that appeals to me is that the game does not have a set time that controls it. In football, basketball and hockey, time is a major factor in strategy and how the game will be played. A team/coach can see the game clock running and knows precisely when the game will end; and much of what is done and why is predicated by the time on the clock.

In baseball there are outs. In a major league game, 27 of them—nine innings with each team getting three outs per inning; in a high school game, 21 outs played over seven innings.

Of course, just as the other sports can go into overtime when the score is tied after regulation, baseball goes into extra innings. In the other sports, again the clock is set for the extra periods of play, and whoever is ahead at the end of the extra period is the victor; in baseball the number of extra innings played is determined by who scores last with the home team always getting the last chance to score if they are tied or behind.

Because there is no clock in baseball, the speed of the game can ebb and flow. Sometimes, in a pitchers' duel, the innings can fly by because nobody is hitting, getting on base or scoring. At other times, the game may seem to drag at a snail's pace because of a pitcher's inability to throw strikes, lots of errors in the field prolonging the inning, many runs being scored, and so on.

Strategically, a coach's job is to maximize his team's use of the outs they have. How much can he and his team produce between outs? What is the best way to maximize your outs? Is it worth it to give up an out for a run early in the game? Should you sacrifice bunt or hit away? Should you attempt to steal a base or hit and run? Defensively, do you bring the infield in to cut off a run or play back for a possible double play?

Whether it is a clock or innings, the point is, how well do you manage what you have to play/work/live with?

Just as there is strategy involved in baseball, there is also strategy in life. The challenge is the same for both: How much can you do with what you are given and what is the best way to maximize what you have within the circumstances that you find yourself, which includes the time you have to do it?

In baseball, if you have an out, you still have hope.

That is the great appeal that this game has for me, and a lesson that can be applied to life—that it ain't over 'til it's over. Baseball is such a game of hope. Anything can happen—and often does—usually in the most tension-filled times. Maybe your team is up by a run or two with only three outs to get. Why does it seem that those three outs are always the toughest three to get? Or maybe you are on the other side of the ledger with your team being down a run or two with three outs to go. Doesn't hope spring eternal if you get a base runner or two on?

Hope simply deals with possibilities. If something is still possible—even in our wildest dreams—if there is still a glimmer of hope, it is worth hanging on to for as long as it exists. That's one of the great lessons that baseball teaches and one that is so applicable to life.

"The essence of optimism is that it takes no account of the present, but it is a source of inspiration, of vitality and **hope** where others have resigned; it enables a man to hold his head high, to claim the future for himself and not to abandon it to his enemy."—*Dietrich Bonhoeffer*

It just ain't over 'til its over!

What Does A Father Say To His Son Before His First Game?

This is your first game, Son. I hope you win.
I hope you win for your sake, not mine, because winning is nice.
It's a good feeling; like the whole world is yours.
But it passes, that feeling. And what lasts is what you've learned.
And what you learn about is Life. That's what sports are all about.
Life.
The whole thing is played out in an afternoon. The happiness of Life.
The miseries. The joys. The heartbreaks.
There's no telling what'll turn up.
There's no telling whether they'll toss you out in the first five minutes
Or whether you'll stay for the long haul.
There's no telling how you'll do.
You might be a hero or you may be absolutely nothing.
There's just no telling. Too much depends on chance–
On how the ball bounces.
I'm not talking about the game, Son. I'm talking about Life.
But it's Life that the game is all about, just as I said.
Because every game is Life; and Life is a game. A serious one.
Dead serious.
But that's what you do with serious things. You do your best.
You take what comes. You take what comes and you run with it.
Winning is fun, sure. But winning is not the point.
Wanting to win is the point. Not giving up is the point.
Never being satisfied with what you've done is the point.
Never letting anyone down is the point.
Play to win, sure.
But play like a champion.
Because it's not winning that counts.
What counts is trying.

—Author Unknown

Hall of Fame Material

End of the season celebrations have been a part of my coaching career since my first year as a coach. Regardless of the type of season we had, there was always a time to recognize the players and positive achievements that inevitably occurred during the season. Sometimes we had to really scratch to find some positives to laud and other times we felt remiss in not being able to give due praise to all for the accomplishments achieved.

From the beginning of my teaching and coaching career, I always felt that there was more to the game than just winning. I had discovered through my own playing days, and had it reinforced as I evolved as a coach and as I studied the lives and techniques of other successful coaches I admired, that winning was a by-product of doing things right. What I came to believe and incorporate into my teaching and coaching philosophy centered around a few basic tenets:

You don't build a man by tearing down a boy.

Everybody has worth and something to offer if given an opportunity to do so.

The most important goal for our players and coaches was to earn the respect of our teammates.

When you build quality people, you build a quality program, and if it's done correctly the results will last a lifetime.

We tried to get away from giving awards that centered solely on an individual's talent but tried to focus on how their performance enhanced the team's performance. Each award, with the exception of the Coaches' award, was voted on by the players. But what we asked them to do was to write reasons why they voted for that person for that particular award. We would compile the votes and the comments and present the awards to the recipients as we shared aloud to the audience the remarks that their teammates had written. We also recognized the other players who had been nominated for the awards by giving them a written compilation of remarks that they had gotten on any of the ballots. We felt that being recognized by even one other teammate for an award was important enough to merit acknowledgment.

Our awards for the most part were pretty typical. We had a Mr. Offense award (for lack of a more imaginative name!) to recognize a player's contributions as a hitter and base runner; a Gold Glove award for our top defender, which could include our pitchers; a Coaches' award presented to the player that the coaches felt best exemplified team spirit, hustle, work ethic, etc. and usually went to a deserving player who perhaps didn't see a great deal of playing time but was invaluable to the team intrinsically; and our capstone award—the one which we placed the greatest significance—the Most Respected Teammate award.

As stated above, our main goal as a team, in fact the only goal that we felt we needed to achieve in order for us to have a successful season, was for each of us to strive to earn the respect of our teammates.

Think about that for a minute.

What do you respect in others? What kind of people/teams do you respect? What kind of effort do you respect? What do you want people to see in you and respect? What do you want people to say and think about you as a person and as a team?

When team members began to answer these questions individually and collectively as a team, the process had begun to build people and a program of respect. Therefore, to be the recipient of the Most Respected Teammate award was to be recognized by your peers not only as a player who had earned their respect, but more importantly, as a person deserving of their respect.

A poem I have often shared with my teams that pretty well sums up this philosophy is by Walt Huntley and is entitled "God's Hall of Fame." It was my hope that all who came under my charge, whether in the classroom or in the athletic arena, would discover, as I had, the joy in the journey to become all that our Creator intended us to be, and to earn self-respect as well as respect from others along the way.

God's Hall of Fame
By Walt Huntley

Your name may not appear down here
In this world's Hall of Fame,
In fact you may be so unknown
That no one knows your name;
The Oscars and the praise of men
May never come your way,
But don't forget God has rewards
That He'll hand out someday.
This Hall of Fame is only good
As long as time shall be;
But keep in mind, God's Hall of Fame
Is for eternity;
To have your name inscribed up there
Is greater more by far

Than all the fame and all the praise
Of every man-made star.
This crowd on earth they soon forget
When you're not up at the top,
They'll cheer like mad until you fall
And then their praise will stop;
Not God, He never does forget,
And in His Hall of Fame,
But just believing in His Son,
Forever—there's your name.
I tell you, friend, I wouldn't trade
My name, however small,
That's written there beyond the stars
In that celestial Hall,
For all the famous names on earth,
Or glory that they share;
I'd rather be an unknown here,
And have my name up there.

“A life is not important
except in the impact
it has on other lives.”

—*Jackie Robinson*

The FUNdaMENTALs of the Game

The way "fundamentals" is spelled in the title is not a typographical error. It was done intentionally to make the point that two major ingredients of fundamentals in anything are that the teaching of them should be "fun" and that they are as much a mental skill as they are physical.

Let me make a couple of important clarifications here. First, my definition of "fun" is "doing things well." When someone says that it doesn't matter about the outcome of a competition as long as everyone has fun, I'm a bit leery. Believe me, it is *not* fun to get blown out of a ball game or humiliated on the field because of ineptitude or poor play! There is a big difference between participating in a game for recreation—just to play—and competing in a game.

A player/team can have "fun" even if they are on the short end of a score provided they know they did things well in the process. They can enjoy the competition pitting their best against somebody else's best. One of my former coaches used to admonish us, "Don't beat yourselves, then try to win." What he was saying was: prepare yourselves well, keep from making avoidable (read as "mental") mistakes, then focus your best effort on playing well. When this occurs, outcomes take care of themselves.

A second clarification centers around the subtle difference between the words fun and enjoyment. It's too bad the word isn't "enjoyamentals" because that would fit my perspective more closely. People like doing things that are fun because it gives them pleasure. The value of the activity is usually that of entertainment. We are entertained by those things that we define as fun. Something fun is usually momentary, pleasurable, and, most often, short term. It's fun to go swimming, go to a dance or to the carnival, etc., because the activities provide entertainment and pleasure to us.

Enjoyment, to me, is something more lasting and long term. Enjoyment implies happiness; fun implies pleasure. A man may enjoy his job even if parts of the job are not necessarily pleasant or fun. I enjoy coaching very much, but having to do fundraising, or inventories or—the worst aspect of coaching—having to make personnel cuts, is neither fun nor pleasurable, but still essential and mandatory parts of the profession. To enjoy something means to accept the whole situation or experience—the pleasant and perhaps the not so pleasant that may be part of it—in its entirety. An overall experience can still be enjoyed and valued even if parts of it were not fun or pleasurable.

Learning the fundamentals of baseball should be both fun and enjoyable. It needs to be fun to maintain interest, especially in youngsters just being introduced to the game, but is important at all levels. I believe teaching the idea that "fun is doing things well" can and should be taught at all levels of the game. With that perspective, baseball becomes both a fun and enjoyable pursuit.

The second part of the word—mental—plays such an important part of the game that now many books and articles are written about it. It doesn't mean that the mental part has just in recent years become important, it is just that more research and interest has led to the understanding of its importance to a greater degree now than in the past. The mental part has always been important though not always understood, nor given its due importance in any aspect of life.

The importance of balance is discussed elsewhere in the book, but nowhere is it more important than in the area of fundamentals. Just as there needs to be a balance between fun and enjoyment, there also needs to be a balance between the body and mind when learning to integrate how the game is played.

> *"'90% of the game is half mental.'*
> *I've said this many times. It's one of my better coaching tips."*
> —Yogi Berra (from the *Yogi Book*)

The question of which comes first or which is more important—the body or the mind—is like asking which came first, the chicken or the egg? I don't think it is useful to get bogged down in that kind of argument. Both are of equal importance, and both have a direct impact on the other.

When you are physically tired or ailing, what is your mental state? Do you have an abundance of optimism, positive thoughts and good feelings? Does your physical condition have an effect on how you view the world on that day? Conversely, if you are feeling great, everything is going well for you physically—doesn't that have an impact on your energy level, perspective and what you feel you can do?

Now, how about your mental state? Have you ever willed yourself to feel better or purposefully refocused your thoughts from how you were feeling to what you needed to do only to discover that when you took your mind off how you felt you were able to accomplish what needed to be done? Proverbs 23:7 states, "As a man thinketh in his heart, so is he." Even thousands of years ago when this was written there was an understanding of the importance of the mental side of the balance equation between the mind and the body.

An important thing to remember about the mind is that it is programmable. It works only on the program, the information that it is fed. It is the most unique computer in the world built by the Ultimate Engineer, and humankind has been attempting for a long time to reproduce it.

We, ourselves, are the programmers who decide what information goes into our minds. That has been the greatest gift from our Creator—the gift of free will—to choose how we want to program our lives. I'm told that computer programmers use the term "GIGO" to refer to how computers ultimately work. "GIGO" stands for "Garbage In-Garbage Out."

If the programmer puts incorrect, useless or misleading information into the computer, the results will be incorrect, useless and misleading—garbage in-garbage out.

Therefore, it seems to me that what is truly important is the information that we program into ourselves. We must ultimately be responsible for "quality control" of what goes into our minds if we are going to be responsible for what comes out—what we become.

Proper fundamentals—of all kinds in all areas of our lives—need to be diligently screened, programmed and practiced, both mentally and physically, in order for us to truly maximize who we can become and to truly have "fun" in all we do.

Ten Rules For Successful Living

By Conrad Hilton

Find your own particular talent.
Be big.
Be honest.
Live with enthusiasm.
Don't let your possessions possess you.
Don't worry about your problems.
Look up to people when you can—down to no one.
Don't cling to the past.
Assume your full share of responsibility in the world.
Pray consistently and confidently.

83% of Winner is INNER

I have always been one who has used little motivational phrases, aphorisms and quotes to help make a point to my students and athletes or possibly to cause them to think about something. I believe that they are helpful as a perspective-giver or to serve as a reminder to get back to or stay on the right track.

Sometimes, in a flash of enlightenment, I may even come up with one myself. The heading for this chapter is one of these.

So much of success in baseball and in life depends upon what a person thinks and believes. Studies have shown that a person's attitude and belief in oneself are more important than one's education or training. Confidence has so much to do with success.

Confidence, simply defined, is one's faith or trust in one's own ability to do something. It also involves a reliance on oneself rather than a dependence upon others to get a job done. Mark Twain said, "All you need in this life is ignorance and confidence, and then success is sure."

Though I may not agree entirely with Mr. Twain's assessment, and I am aware that it was meant to be taken with a liberal grain of salt, there is some truth to it. As a teacher, I learned long ago that you never want to tell a student s/he can't do something because it may discourage them from even trying. My advice, when a student has expressed to me a dream or desire that they have, is "Good for you. Go for it!" Over my career I have seen many students and athletes achieve more than many people believed they would or could simply because they had—and listened to—a little voice inside them that said that they could.

That's where "83% of Winner is Inner" came from. Though I'm no mathematician, I did figure out that "inner" comprises 5/6, or in decimal form .83, of the word "winner." After reading many sports psychology experts and their take on the importance of the mental or inner game, I thought that would be a fairly catchy way to explain this importance to my players (and students).

It has been said that confidence is a plant of slow growth. As such, it takes much care and nurturing. It can be easily damaged or extinguished if left unattended or if criticism is too caustic or overused. Confidence is nourished by outside sources through sincere compliments, pats on the back and positive recognition from others. But more importantly, it must be something that each individual attends to oneself.

How is that accomplished?

I think three C's provides a large part of the answer: Concentration–Conviction–Courage.

Concentration is another term for focus, which is necessary if you want to accomplish your objective. One's goal must be clearly in focus—and in living color!—before it can be accomplished. When one has a clear, concise road map to where they want to go, they can head there with confidence.

Conviction is the strong belief not only in what you are doing—that it is good and right—but also that you are deserving of accomplishing what you have set out to do. When a person is convinced that their mission is worthy and that an honest effort is being made to achieve it, there is usually a sense of righteous confidence accompanying it.

The third C, Courage, emanates from the other C's. The word courage comes from the Latin word, cor, which means heart. Courage, then, is literally putting your heart into that which you believe and going forth toward doing what it takes to fulfill it.

These three C's—and the Confidence which flows from them—are all found within us. They are there to be developed, and like any other skill or characteristic, must be honed and used or they will atrophy and die. Someone may help us to discover these or we may discover them within ourselves by ourselves through our experience. The important thing is that once they are discovered and used, we are 83% closer to being a winner!

If I Had A Boy

If I had a boy, I would say to him, "Son,
Be fair and be square in the race you must run;
Be brave if you lost and be meek if you win,
Be better and nobler than I've ever been;
Be honest and fearless in all that you do
And honor the name I have given you."
If I had a boy, I'd want him to know
We reap in this life just about what we sow.
And we get what we earn, be it little or great,
Regardless of luck and regardless of fate;
I would teach him and show him the best that I could
That it pays to be honest and upright and good.
I would make him a pal and a partner of mine
And show him the things in this world that are fine;
I would show him the things that are wicked and bad,
For I figure this knowledge should come from his Dad;
I would walk with him, talk with him, play with him, too,
And to all of my promises strive to be true.
We would grow up together and I'd be a boy,
And share in his troubles and share in his joy;
We would work out problems together and then
We would lay out our plans when we both would be men;
And, oh, what a joy it would be,
No pleasure in life could be greater to me.

—*Author Unknown*

A Tour of the Bases—In the Dugout

"A journey of a thousand miles begins with a single step."
—Lao Tse

One of the annual teaching plans for my teams each season is called the tour of the bases. The tour is intended to cover the basic fundamentals of base running as well as introduce some of the finer points of the game. It is usually conducted over a period of days because of the amount of things to cover and "sights to see" along the way. Just as a feast is eaten one bite at a time, it is best to break down the tour into smaller segments so that all the information is "digested" as well. All is important and will enhance their knowledge and application of the game.

For many players, this is the first time that anyone has taken the time to give them a complete and thorough tour of the bases. Many have heard portions of what the tour will discuss, but few have had it put into context as it is done on the tour. The intent is to provide an overview—the big picture—of the game as well as to explain how the various segments of the game fit together to make up the big picture.

Although the tour is predominately conducted on the diamond, it is, as with many trips, begun with preplanning, which, in this case, begins in the dugout.

Good base running, good offense, good defense, game strategy—all these things begin long before a team takes the field to play. Not counting the hours spent in practice to prepare for a game, additional preparation prior to a game is necessary. A savvy coach and his team are going to check out the conditions of the field. How are the baselines raked and watered? Will it be fast or slow? What is the condition of the infield and outfield—is it rough or will it play true hops? Is the grass long or short? How will the ball carom off the walls and backstop? How is the wind blowing—which direction/how hard? What are the ground rules for this field? There are many considerations to account for regarding the playing field, let alone how to prepare for, and take advantage of, the other team and any possible weaknesses that they may display.

While in the dugout prior to the game, intent players are watching the opposition take infield. They are watching how the infielders and outfielders play the field—especially if it's the opponent's home field—to possibly learn where and how they should play the field. They should be watching for weaknesses or irregularities that the opposition may show during their practice time, i.e. weak arms or poor fundamentals that may be taken advantage of during the game.

If possible, they should watch the opposing pitcher warm up. What is he throwing? How consistently is he throwing all his pitches for strikes? What is his arm angle? Does he change speeds on his pitches? Does he telegraph his pitches by slowing his motion down or changing his delivery?

All these things, and more, are talked about at the beginning of the tour of the bases—and we haven't even left the dugout yet! The point here, obviously, is that there is a great deal of preparation and there are lots of things going on in baseball that many fans, and unfortunately some players, are unaware of. The people and teams that are consistently successful are ones that pay attention to detail. They take care of business—the great and the mundane—with equal attention. Anything that may affect the performance of the team or the outcome of the contest is important, and therefore worthy of attention. A coach or team can't control any of the factors discussed above, but they should acquire as much knowledge as they can that may be beneficial to them when playing the game.

This important part of a team's preparation marks the beginning of the tour of the bases. It not only provides important information needed to know prior to when a team leaves the dugout to play defense, but provides each player with information that will help him as he begins what he hopes will be a successful trip around the bases when it's his team's turn to try to score some runs.

"To finish the moment, to find the journey's end in every step of the road, to live the greatest number of good hours, is wisdom."

—*Emerson*

A Tour of the Bases—On Deck and Batter's Box

"A full head is an empty bat."
—Branch Rickey

Our first stop after leaving the dugout, offensively, is to go to the on-deck circle where a hitter awaits his turn at bat. This needs to be a productive time for the hitter, not a time to chat with fans or scope out the crowd. It is a time to get both physically, mentally and emotionally prepared to face the pitcher.

Many hitters limber up by swinging a weighted bat and stretching. Good hitters are also studying the pitcher from a closer distance to discern ball velocity, movement, location, and accuracy. Again, he is checking to see if the pitcher may be tipping his pitches in some way such as changing arm angle or slowing his delivery. This is a time to also check out how the catcher and pitcher are working together to get hitters out. Have they fallen into a pattern of pitches that they are using on every batter, i.e. starting off each hitter with a fastball or breaking pitch?

The hitter is also thinking about the situation he will find himself in at the plate. What will his job be? Is he the leadoff hitter or batting with no one on base? Will he be called upon to bunt, protect the runner by swinging through a pitch, hit and run? The situation of the game often determines what a hitter's job will be, though ultimately it boils down to trying to make hard contact with the ball, unless he is called upon to bunt.

All these thoughts and preparations, including getting into a state that I refer to as "relaxed concentration"—being totally focused on the task at hand while controlling the body's tension level to allow it (the body) to perform most efficiently—occur prior to stepping into the batter's box. Once a hitter steps into the box the time for thinking is over; now it is a time for action!

As Branch Rickey's quote at the top of the page suggests, if a hitter is worried about whether he's holding his bat correctly, or what his batting average is, or whether or not he is going to get hit by the ball or anything else other than "see the ball—hit the ball," he is doomed for failure. The total focus of a hitter's existence at this particular moment in his life is the **ball**. Nothing else is important. It is the hitter facing his ultimate opponent—the ball.

Note that I purposefully focus on the ball as the ultimate opponent, not the pitcher, or the other team. The ball. A player must hit It, catch It, throw It, beat It to the base on offense or have It beat the runner there when playing defense. The inanimate ball—something with no feelings or emotions, totally unbiased and impartial—is ultimately what we are playing against. Once we recognize what, not who, it is that we are playing against, it is easier to stay focused on what we are trying to do when playing the game. The ball, then, becomes our focal point to bring us back under emotional control in times of distress that inevitably occur during the course of a game.

Great players understand the old axiom, "If you fail to prepare, you prepare to fail." They do all they can to be prepared physically, mentally and emotionally to play the game—day in and day out. They understand what they have control of and what they don't, and conduct themselves accordingly. They learn to be prepared for what may happen but learn to live in the "here and now." They focus on the task at hand and do not become concerned with all the "what ifs" that may occur.

Great players tend to be optimistic in their approach and are truly thankful just for the opportunity to play the game they are so passionate about. They take nothing for granted and play every game as if it were their last. They try to play so that they will have no regrets when they are done playing, especially in terms of their effort and preparation.

To paraphrase an old commercial, "An at-bat is a terrible thing to waste." As players, we just don't know for sure how many at-bats we are going to get in our careers. That's why it is so important to make every one count, to be as prepared as we possibly can to make the most of the opportunities that arise, and to be able to do what we are called upon to do when it's our turn.

How well we prepare will have a bearing on how successful we will ultimately be getting out of the batter's box and heading on the first leg of our tour—to first base.

"Never let the fear of striking out get in your way."

—*Babe Ruth*

Tour of the Bases—Heading Toward First

This segment is entitled "heading toward first" instead of "heading to first" for a specific reason. What a hitter does at bat is going to determine whether he is heading to—or toward—first base. If the hitter knows he has hit a ball out of the infield, he will head toward first base with the idea of rounding it and being headed toward second base. In the event that the ball is in the gap or is misplayed by the outfielder, this will allow for an extra base to be taken.

Hitters–turned–base runners should have the mentality of being *held* to a base rather than just settling for getting to a base. I want my players to be *held* to a single by the defense rather than just settling for a single without putting pressure on the defense.

If the hitter draws a base on balls or hits the ball to an infielder who has a play at first, the hitter/runner should run hard *to* (actually straight through the bag when the ball is hit) first with the idea of stopping there.[4]

When the ball is hit and there will be a play at first base, the first task for the hitter/runner is to get out of the batter's box as quickly as possible. As with every other action in the game, there is a proper technique to doing so. Regardless of whether the batter is left- or right-handed, after the completion of the swing, the hitter-turned-runner should take his initial step toward first base with his back foot (right foot for the right-handed batter, left foot for the left-handed batter). This is the case because the momentum of the swing allows for the quickest exit from the box being with the back leg and foot.

Upon leaving the batter's box, the runner is running in a straight line to first with his eyes on the edge of the base facing him (it is acceptable for a runner to glance in toward the infield quickly to see where the ball is and if it is being fielded; if by chance it gets through the infield, his route to first will change). He runs with good mechanical form and with a loose jaw and hands to control tension. When he gets to the bag he runs through it, touching the front edge of the bag with whichever foot is in the lead while not chopping, lunging or breaking stride to do so, and leaning his chest through the bag as if he were breaking the tape at the end of a race.

After he crosses the bag, he quickly glances over his right shoulder to see if the ball has been overthrown, which may allow him to advance to second base. Just after crossing the bag, he breaks down his sprint with a series of choppy steps, and, if the ball has been overthrown, may decide to run directly to second base. If the ball has not been overthrown, he will return to the base immediately, unless of course he has been called out by the umpire.

If the ball has gone through the infield or has been hit into the outfield, the route to first will be much different than if it had been hit to an infielder. Upon leaving the batter's box in the same fashion as when the ball was hit in the infield—with the back foot first—the runner wants to position himself so as to be heading in a straight line to second base as he runs toward first with the intention of "rounding" first and head toward second. He can run this route to position himself in two ways.

First, he can start to make an arc when leaving the batter's box that will allow him to touch the inside corner of the first base bag while leaning in hard and positioning himself in a straight line toward second. Baseball is a game of angles and arcs and successful teams know what the correct angles and arcs are and how and when to use them. This is one of those times.

The second way for the runner to position himself in a straight line toward second base is to run a "question mark" when approaching first base. When the runner leaves the batter's box, he runs directly toward first (as if the ball had been hit to an infielder). When he reaches approximately 70 feet down the first base line, he veers right, out of the base line, then leans in hard left to hit the inside corner of the first base bag and be in line with second base. The route he takes looks as if he has drawn a question mark through the first base bag.

Again, the idea here is to put pressure on the defense to handle the ball well and do things right or else we will take advantage of mistakes they make. We must be held to first otherwise we will advance when the opportunity arises.

There are so many parallels between running the bases and life. First, it is very helpful to "get off on the right (correct) foot" when getting started. We must know what our goal is and have our eyes fixed on where we are headed—with an occasional glance around to see if the situation has changed which may alter our goal. We must know that the "shortest distance between two points is a straight line" and act accordingly when time is of the essence. On the other hand, sometimes we may need to alter our route so as to put us in a better position to take advantage of opportunities along the way. We must anticipate opportunities so as to be prepared for them when they do arise. Finally, we must always put forth our best effort in all stages—planning-preparation-performance—because our best effort equals our best chance to succeed.

Now that we have made it safely to our first goal in our journey, we need to know the best way to proceed to get ourselves in to scoring position, which would be the next possible stop on our tour—second base.

"The secret of getting ahead is getting started.
The secret of getting started is breaking your complex overwhelming tasks into small manageable tasks, and then starting on the first one."

—*Mark Twain*

Tour of the Bases—Second Base—Scoring Position

"Progress always involves risk; you can't steal second base and keep your foot on first."

—Frederick Wilcox

Second base is referred to as the "keystone" because of its importance to both the offensive and defensive teams.

Offensively, second base is important because it is considered scoring position, meaning that most of the time, on a base hit to the outfield, the runner at second will have the opportunity to score. Therefore, a large part of offensive strategy is to get runners to, and hopefully, past second base. With a runner on first, the offense may elect to try to steal second, bunt a runner to second, employ a hit and run or run and hit strategies—all for the purpose of moving the runner closer to the eventual destination: home.

Defensively, a team is trying to keep the offense from getting to second base because it is in scoring position, but also because, with a runner on first, the defense still has a force play at second and, with less than two outs with a runner on first, an opportunity to turn a double play—two outs on a single ball hit to an infielder who relays it to second then to first before the runners arrive to those bases. A double play is what is referred to as a "pitcher's best friend."

Second base is half way home. There are still two legs of the journey to complete—touching third and making it home. Success in baseball is measured by how often this tour of the bases occurs during a game, i.e. runs score, and only matters (to those keeping score) if your team scores more than the opposition. "You've got to touch 'em all" if you're going to score in baseball.

One thing a base runner has to guard against, regardless of the base he occupies, is getting picked off by the pitcher or catcher throwing to the base before the runner can get back to it safely. The base is, in a sense, a safe haven for the runner occupying it, and if he is careless, he can be "put out" by the defensive team thus taking away the chance to possibly add to his team's score.

A key to successful base running is good judgment. Good judgment comes from experience, knowledge, a sense of anticipation, awareness of the situation and an understanding of game and management strategy. It is an understanding of when—and when not—to take risks on the bases. It is responding[5] confidently, efficiently, prudently and quickly to what the situation—or the opposition—presents.

It has been said that "good judgment comes from experience, and experience comes from bad judgment." In large measure, this is true, especially as it pertains to baseball and base running specifically. Sometimes the runner must rely on his own instincts and judgment and at other times he has the aid of base coaches who can assist him on the journey.

Obviously, trust in someone else's judgment, then, becomes a factor in the decision-making process which brings us back to the whole concept of teamwork. At times, bad judgment due to poor preparation (e.g. not knowing the strength of the outfielders' arms), desperation (e.g. team has been struggling and a player or coach tries to "make something happen"), or not reading the situation correctly (e.g. thinking that the runner was faster than he actually was for the situation), happens. Occasionally, you get lucky, the bad judgment doesn't cost you and you may still learn a valuable lesson on top of it. Most of the time, however, bad judgment costs us dearly, and hopefully, we can turn the experience into one that we learn from and will benefit us in the future.

I believe that experience can come from good judgment as well, though perhaps the greatest lessons we learn are from the most painful ones. Costing your team a run because of poor base running—especially when you are in scoring position—is an experience most players (and coaches) have had if they have been around the game for any length of time. But it is a result of these experiences that cause players to grow and get better. Adversity, when viewed from a healthy perspective, can make us stronger if it is not allowed to defeat us.

The important thing to remember here is that we must be quick learners and learn from the mistakes that we make—as well as from the mistakes of others—without having to repeat them (too often!). When we can learn from our mistakes, and not get picked off as a result of them, we have an opportunity to continue our journey around the bases—rounding third and heading for home!

"You start with a bag full of luck and an empty bag of experience. The trick is to fill the bag of experience before you empty the bag of luck. Good judgment comes from experience. Unfortunately, the experience usually comes from bad judgment."

—*Unknown*

Tour of the Bases—Rounding Third and Heading for Home

"Stopping at third base adds no more to the score than striking out."

—Billy Sunday

There are nine ways to score from third base with less than 2 outs and without the bases being loaded:

1. infield out
2. error
3. squeeze play
4. steal of home
5. hit
6. wild pitch
7. passed ball
8. balk
9. fly ball

Second base is considered scoring position, but a runner is only going to score from there in a couple of ways: either by a base hit (single, double, triple or home run), an error, or, depending on the runner, the length of the fly ball and the defense, possibly a two-base sacrifice fly, which doesn't occur very often at all.

So when a runner makes it to third base, especially with less than two outs, his chance of adding a run to his team's score has increased dramatically. To not score when in this situation is one of the most frustrating things that can happen to a team and can cause a great momentum shift in the game. What a downer for the offensive team and what an upper for the defense!

The runner at third base must be alert for many things. The third base coach is right there to remind him of many of these things such as the number of outs, what to do when and if the ball is put into play,[6] to lead off in foul territory in the event that a batted ball may hit him (if the runner is in fair territory when a ball hits him, he would be out; if it hits him when he is in foul territory, it is only a foul ball), as well as to lend encouragement.

However, it is the runner himself, who must get the job done. It is he who is responsible for getting the good jump to try to score or reading the situation to determine whether or not to get into a rundown if the ball beats him to the plate or try to dislodge the ball from the catcher's grasp. Again, it comes down to good judgment and experience to take advantage of the scoring opportunity from third base.

"Heading for home" conjures up many emotions both related and unrelated to baseball. Is it a coincidence that home plate is actually shaped like a house?

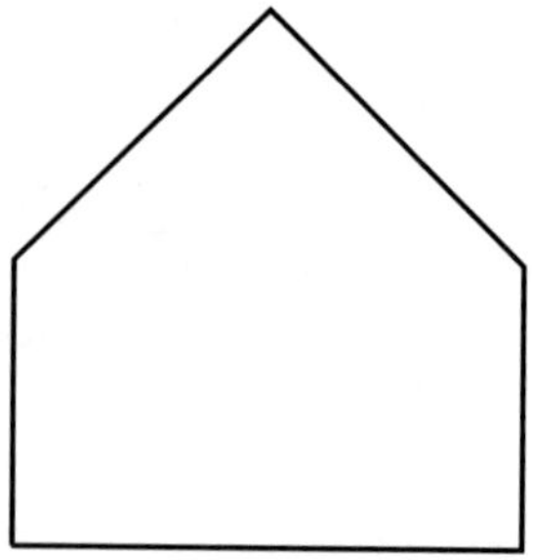

Coming home after a journey of considerable distance and perhaps some peril is always a comforting experience. Often, we are greeted there by others who are happy to see us and celebrate our return with us. There is usually a sense of well-being and accomplishment upon our return to home.

In essence, "home" signifies everything that we desire or work for. It is what gives meaning to baseball as well as life. It provides a purpose, goal, and a mission. To fall short of reaching home is to feel a sense of incompletion—a sense that something is missing. As Billy Sunday, former major league baseball player turned preacher of the early 20th century expressed in the quote at the beginning of this section, stopping at third adds nothing to the score.

Baseball provides such a great opportunity to teach about life's important lessons. The tour of the bases is just one example of baseball as a metaphor for life. It encompasses so many parallels between the two—the importance of good judgment, perspective, experience, anticipation, dealing with emotional highs and lows, good breaks and bad breaks, teamwork, camaraderie, winning and losing.

Is it any wonder why baseball has been called our national pastime?

"Home is a place you grow up wanting to leave, and grow old wanting to get back to."

—John Ed Pearce

Passion—There IS Crying in Baseball

". . . Are you crying? There's no crying in baseball!"
—Jimmy Dugan from A League of Their Own

My apologies to Tom Hanks' character, Jimmy Dugan, but yes, there is crying in baseball, just as there is crying in virtually all aspects of life where people can become emotionally involved—passionate.

Can you imagine what life would be like without emotion? Would you want to live in such a world? Even though emotions are a mixed bag, with some leading to good and pleasant experiences and others leading to trouble, I'm sure I would rather take the bad with the good rather than to have none at all. Wouldn't you?

The word emotion means to be moved by strong feelings. The word passion comes from the Latin word meaning to endure. Is it any wonder, then, why these two words are so often linked? Strong feelings, desires and passions do endure for a long time within us, and the more powerful the emotions, the longer we endure them.

Why is it, or how is it, that someone can become so emotionally attached to a game? These questions have been asked of me by my wife for close to 35 years. I mumble something to her about it being an outgrowth of teaching—my laboratory where I can help build young men—as I kiss her goodbye on my way to practice or a game. I don't think she completely accepts my feeble explanation nor fully understands the idea that perhaps, I, myself, don't have a thorough grasp of why I have such a passion for the game either.

Now, I can understand with some certainty the passion = endurance part. Baseball is a game of long-suffering, and if one doesn't have endurance to get over the hard times, bad hops, bad luck, failure-at-the-rate-of-70%-or-better hitting, and all the other things that happen that try one's patience, they won't last long in the game. "Sports," said John Wooden, "do not build character. They reveal it."

What I'm not so sure I have an answer for is why the emotional attachment? What is it about the game that would cause my wife to see it as competition, to her, perhaps greater than another woman? "Sometimes I think you love baseball more than me because you spend more time with it than you do me," she has uttered more than once over the years. To be truthful she is probably right—about the time spent, that is. Tears have been shed (mostly by her) over baseball, for a variety of reasons.

When our sons and daughter played in their first games, there was crying. When they played their final games in high school, there was crying. When championships were won—or lost—there was crying. When our youngest son was drafted by the Pittsburgh Pirates out of high school and left home shortly after his graduation to begin his professional career in baseball, there was crying. When we saw him play major league baseball for the first time, there was crying. We have been blessed with many other happenings in our lives that have caused displays of emotion that could be chronicled here in addition to the ones involving playing or coaching. (Okay, not all of the crying throughout all these adventures was just my wife . . .)

People need to feel emotion and passion to feel alive. I cannot think of any time I have felt more alive than on the baseball field, either as a player or coach. (This is not to say that I haven't felt alive in other aspects of my life—like my marriage!) Those things in life that we can become passionate about, that we can show emotions for, are the true essence of life.

Let me clarify something here. Emotions are truly important in our lives, but they must not go unchecked nor be the controlling element that dictates our behavior. Emotions must be controlled and channeled so as to be beneficial rather than detrimental in our behavior and in our association with others. They, like many other natural elements such as fire and water, left unchecked, can be catastrophic in their damage to self and others. However, when channeled or contained they add greatly to the depth and warmth of the life experience.

So, sorry, Jimmy Dugan, I can't agree with you. There is crying in baseball. Moreover, I think it is a good thing. And I think that the reasons for crying in baseball are justifiable simply because, as it has been the theme of this book, baseball is simply a metaphor for life, and life should be experienced to the fullest—including crying now and then.

"They give you a round bat, and they throw you a round ball, and they tell you to hit it square."

—*Willie Stargell*

The Five Tool Player

There are five skills or "tools" in baseball that all players (excluding pitchers) are judged by. These are hit for average, hit with power, run, throw, and field. A player who can do all these things at an above average level is considered a five tool player. At the major league level one can find a greater number of these types of players than at any other level, but still they are a rare breed. Very few players are true five tool players and as players get older and skills diminish even fewer stay five tool players over an extended period of time. Those who do are in the Hall of Fame.

Most players may be strong in a couple of these areas but it usually takes above average proficiency in at least two or three areas for players to continue to advance. Rarely do you see a person with outstanding ability in one area advance consistently unless it is a player with a great arm who can be developed as a pitcher. Hitting is of secondary importance to a pitcher, as is his running speed. Hopefully, he is at least an average fielder. But if he can throw . . .

The advent of the designated hitter in baseball in the early '70's was designed to give players with the exceptional ability of hitting a chance to stay in the game longer. It was also a position where a player whose skills in other areas were waning could prolong his career so long as he could still hit. The American League in Major League Baseball allows for the designated hitter while the National League does not. It has prolonged the careers of many great players, and in fact, has become a specialty position in baseball for hitters just as the long reliever or closers have become to pitching.

Just as there are five tools in baseball that provide for a well-rounded and balanced player, there are five areas in our personal lives that need to be developed and balanced as well. These are the physical, emotional, intellectual, social and spiritual dimensions of our lives, and how well we do in developing and balancing these areas has much to do with our happiness and well-being in life.

It is only natural for baseball players to focus on those aspects of the game that they do well or want to do well in. Most players love to hit and spend a great deal of time hitting because it is something that they can do, to a large degree, by themselves. Hitters can go to automated batting cages or hit off batting tees into a net for hours at a time. It may be more fun to hit "live" which means having somebody rather than a pitching machine throw to you, and perhaps is more beneficial because it is closer to how the game is really played. But how much can a player work on his defensive ability by himself? (Besides, who signs the big contracts—the guys who can hit, or the guys who can field? The bat is mightier than the glove where the big money is concerned.)

It is equally as natural for people to do those things that they are most comfortable with in other areas of their lives. Often, we do not pay attention to certain areas until they are way out of balance and things begin to break down. Perhaps we spend long hours developing our minds through reading, study, classes, and so on, but neglect our physical and social dimensions until our bodies or our relationships with others begin to suffer. Or maybe we spend most of our time developing our physical side to the exclusion of the other dimensions. Regardless of which dimension we focus upon, if the others are being significantly excluded or ignored, we will become out of balance in our lives and our total well-being will be affected.

There are two important points to consider here. First, that it is very important to be as well-rounded and balanced as possible. Second, it requires other people to help us become as well-rounded and balanced as we can.

Just as it takes awareness, dedication, work and the assistance of others to develop all five tools in baseball, it takes the same to develop all five dimensions of our selves. The big difference between these two areas is that with the personal dimensions, all areas are much more intertwined and interdependent with each other than the five tools of a baseball player. Though the five tools in baseball may have a bearing on each other to some degree and can be influenced by factors such as strength, conditioning and overall talent, the five dimensions of our lives are much more dependent on each other to maintain balance.

As it has been stated earlier, it is possible for a player to "get by" fairly well with a couple or a few of the tools and become reasonably successful. But in regard to our personal dimensions, a greater development of each of these areas is required for people to be truly happy and have a balanced life.

A song from the Broadway musical *Funny Girl* expresses the sentiment "People who need people are the luckiest people in the world." The five dimensions of our selves, though an individual choice to develop them within ourselves, often requires the assistance and participation of others for them to be fully developed within us. Humans are social animals who are stimulated physically, emotionally, intellectually, socially and spiritually by others. We need others to help meet these needs.

Even though we can work out on our own, or read a book, or meditate or have quality time by ourselves, we can't reach our fullest potential as human beings unless we share ourselves with others and allow others to share themselves with us. Just as all players know that there is a big difference between practice and game time, there is a great difference in trying to develop our selves by ourselves and developing our selves through the interaction with others.

Becoming a five tool player in baseball may be out of reach for most players who play, but becoming a five dimensional person is not out of reach for any of us if we understand what the dimensions are, understand the importance of keeping them all in balance, and look for opportunities to involve others in the development of them in our lives. Becoming a five dimensional player over an extended period of time (our lifetime) should get us into a special Hall of Fame as well.

"Why certainly I'd like to have that fellow who hits a home run every time at bat, who strikes out every opposing batter when he's pitching, who throws strikes to any base or the plate when he's playing outfield and who's always thinking about two innings ahead just what he'll do to baffle the other team. Any manager would want a guy like that playing for him. The only trouble is to get him to put down his cup of beer and come down out of the stands and do those things."

—Danny Murtaugh
Former manager, Pittsburgh Pirates

Team Chemistry = Harmony + Balance

"The two most important words in life are love and balance."

—John Wooden

Much is made about the importance of team or group chemistry and its role in the overall success of an organization. Many believe that it just happens—that when a team does have a good chemistry and teammates get along, it's kind of the luck of the draw.

I don't think so. I believe that team chemistry is something that can be developed and should be part of the primary mission of the organization, whether that organization is a team, a business, a club or a family unit. I further believe that the leader of the organization—the coach, the boss, the president or the parent(s)—is ultimately responsible for the development of this important ingredient.

Using the words team and chemistry together has always fascinated me. Team is discussed at length elsewhere in this book, so I won't address it much here accept to offer the definition that a true team is comprised of a collection of individuals who consciously make the choice to put the mission and goals of the group above their own personal goals. The acrostic for TEAM—**T**ogether **E**veryone **A**chieves **M**ore—epitomizes this notion well.

Chemistry involves the mixing—or taking away—of components or elements to form yet another "solution." A chemist is knowledgeable about reactions when various chemicals are mixed together and very careful when mixing ingredients—especially unknown ones—together. S/he is usually working toward a "solution" to a question or problem that has been the focus of attention. Sometimes it is even found that one can add to the (final) solution by actually taking away an ingredient that is not mixing well with the other properties.

The leader of a group is the "head chemist" when it comes to putting the group together. S/he must have in mind what the mission and goals will be and what kind of "solution" it will take to accomplish them. Often, the leader has to use the ingredients provided him/her in the people that comprises the group. Sometimes it is possible to add or subtract some of these components; sometimes the leader must experiment with what is available to build a solution that can be successful.

Having been a leader in a number of the groups listed above (team, club, family) over the course of my lifetime, I have concluded that in order to have Team Chemistry, the ingredients of Harmony and Balance must be present. Without them, you don't have a team but rather a collection of individuals wearing the same uniform or a group of individuals with the same group name.

Harmony is defined as "the pleasing agreement of parts." In other words, the parts fit together well; they get along. To put it in human relationship terms, people care about each other and go out of their way to blend their talents, goals and personalities with others for the benefit of all. Harmony in music adds a richness and depth to the composition that far surpasses just the melody. People who blend together their talents in a synergistic way far surpass what a single individual or group of individuals not working together, can accomplish. And just as a beautiful harmonic piece of music can stir the soul and inspire one to great things, so it is with a group of people who blend together with common purpose. Harmony, when it reaches this level, could equate to the love alluded to in the quote by John Wooden at the beginning of this chapter.

Balance has a number of interesting meanings that apply to this context: "equilibrium; stability, harmonious proportion of elements." All structures require balance—in all their dimensions—to sustain themselves. A tire that is out of balance wears unevenly and rides roughly until, eventually, it breaks down. When a tire is unbalanced, it affects the other parts of the machine to which it is a part, and can begin a chain reaction that eventually leads to the total breakdown of the machine.

A group must see itself as a collection of parts that are not necessarily equal in talent or responsibility but cannot function effectively as a total group without the contributions of all parts working together. In other words, what good is it to have a Lamborghini, if you don't have the little key to start it? What good is it to have a great home run hitter if nobody else gets on base or the team has no pitching to hold down the opponent's offense? What good is it to have great pitching but the inability to score runs?

Part of being the "head chemist" is getting the individual members of the group to understand and accept this important concept. The overall success of the group depends upon it.

A few years back, Hillary Clinton said that "it takes a village to raise a child." In essence, she was talking about team chemistry. It takes everybody working together for the same purpose—with the understanding that all will benefit if everyone's talents are pooled together—to achieve what the group is capable of achieving.

Harmony and balance—they are what makes the world go 'round . . . smoothly!

“Happiness is not a matter of intensity but of balance and order and rhythm and harmony.”

—*Thomas Merton*

The Ripple Effect

Throughout my teaching and coaching career I have used the following analogy:

"Go down to the lake and pick up a handful of rocks, pebbles and sand and throw it into the water. What do you see?"

Invariably, my students answer that they see ripples on the water.

I go on to explain that the size of the ripples are determined by the size of the object that hits the water, but regardless of the size of the object, each creates a ripple that goes on to intersect with other ripples in an ever-widening circle.

There are a couple of points I am trying to make with this lesson. First, there is no such thing as an insignificant life. Regardless of the size of the splash we make, our life is going to make an impact on the lives of others as our ripple grows and ever expands from its starting point. And the longer we live, the larger our ripple circle becomes, and the more people we will affect throughout our lives. The size of the splash, and therefore the breadth of our ripple, depends upon what we do with our lives. We can create a wave that may reach a great distance and impact many, or a ripple that may not reach quite as far but is still no less significant to the ones closest to us.

The second point is that our lives will have an impact on innumerable people who we will never know ourselves. I explain that they are being influenced by people they will never know through me—by my family members, and teachers and coaches and friends—all the people who have made an impression on me and who have helped to make me who I am are affecting them because I am affecting them. Their life ripples are colliding with ripples that have emanated perhaps long before and quite some distance from where they are, and theirs, in turn, will have an impact on others in the same way.

When I reflect on how I teach and coach, I am constantly reminded of how much of an impact others have made on the way I do things. Phrases I use in coaching are ones I've picked up from coaches whom I have played for, worked with or studied. Stories and lessons taught to me—either through my formal education at school or through the informal education from my family, friends or experiences—that are shared with my students and athletes that I believe to be instructive, are more examples of the ripple effect.

Nature can be so instructive—so alliterative—in its lessons if we just look for the lessons within it. We see what we look for. A big part of education is learning the importance of this. Learning how to see things, and understanding that we will see what we are looking for—in other words gaining perspective—are two of the most important tools we can learn to use in school to prepare us for life. Life is natural, and it only stands to reason that by really studying natural things, we can learn so much. As Yogi Berra said, "You can observe a lot by watching."

Baseball has always been a tool that I have tried to use to explain some of these life concepts to my players. How a player (or coach) reacts to a bad call can have an impact on his teammates or team. It can cause them to lose focus on the important task at hand or focus upon that which will only be detrimental to them. We are most effective when we are concentrating on one thing at a time. If we have taken our focus off what we are trying to accomplish, or if we try to split our attention, we lose our effectiveness and also our momentum toward that goal. We control what we look at or how we are going to allow something to affect us. It is very important that we also recognize that our reactions can, and usually will, have an affect on others.

Understanding the ripple effect and applying it to our lives is one of the most insightful and important lessons that we can learn. To know that we are significant, that we can and do make a difference in the world, and the kind of difference that we make is in our own hands, empowers us to become all we that we can become.

It's time to make a splash!

"It is not the honor that you take with you,
but the heritage you leave behind."

—*Branch Rickey*

"Fleece 'Em" and "Ferocious Gentlemen"

Many years ago when I was a rookie coach in my first year of teaching and coaching at the high school level, I took a baseball coaching class and chanced to meet a wonderful "old" coach who had been coaching for over 40 years. He was most gracious in sharing some of his materials with me as well as being very encouraging to "a rook."

What a gold mine that was and what a wonderful gift Coach Lee Sonnedecker shared with me at that time! Coach Sonnedecker was "old school" in his approach to coaching. By his material, I could tell instantly that he was teaching more than the game of baseball. Rather, he was teaching his young men life skills through baseball—the correct way to do things from how to wear a uniform to what it means to be a teammate to how to conduct themselves on and off the field. He had clear expectations and the know-how to carry it out. He had been a highly successful coach over the years with well-disciplined teams that fared very well in the won-lost column as well.

One of the concepts that he shared with me which I immediately adopted for my own fledging program was the notion of fielding a team of "ferocious gentlemen." He explained that what he expected from his players—during practice as well as games—was that they would be very intense, aggressive, unyielding in their approach to the game, but that they would always be sportsmen and gentlemen who played hard but always by, and within, the scope of the rules.

I liked that! I really liked how he had chosen just the precise words to identify exactly what his expectations were for his players. It was very easy for them (and for me!) to visualize and understand what and how he expected them to conduct themselves. What I also liked about the concept was its carryover value off the field and its application to all other areas of life.

Ferocious gentlemen. Live life large and with gusto, but live it within the parameters of decency and respect for others. What a wonderful model I was so fortunate to be introduced to so early in my coaching and teaching career! No wonder Coach Sonnedecker, when he retired from teaching and coaching, was honored as he was.

Later in my career, I had my first opportunity to coach girls. At the time, I was the varsity baseball coach and varsity girls' basketball coach at a fairly large high school. I had plenty of experience coaching both sports—but no experience coaching girls. And what an experience it was . . . once I understood that coaching girls wasn't exactly like coaching boys. This experience was in the early '80's and, though the girls' basketball team had been established just a few years earlier, it was still a fledgling program comprised of a few decent athletes but with very little basketball knowledge or experience.

What these tremendous young ladies lacked in talent, experience and knowledge, they made up for with a willingness to learn, good effort and enthusiasm . . . most of the time. Because girls' athletics was relatively new at the time—Title IX was just kicking in—our girls didn't always have the same perspective about sports and training as boys had so long been accustomed to. It was a major challenge to get them to understand at that time that basketball was a contact sport—that it was not only okay to bump other players in the course of the game, sometimes that bumping was intentional and necessary in order to play the game the way it was meant to be played.

This is where "Fleece 'em" came into existence. I often use acrostics with my teams to help them remember things I want them to remember. "Fleece" was an acrostic for "**F**erocious **L**adies, **E**ffort, **E**nthusiasm, **C**lass, **E**veryone." Now, the fact that the word "fleece" also had a meaning of "taking something from another" e.g. "I've been fleeced," would mean that somebody had something taken from them, or that they had been taken advantage of—fit nicely with our focus on playing a tough, in-your-face defense that we were trying to teach. Therefore, we broke all our huddles with "Fleece 'em!"

Though we did not have a winning record over the two years that I was the girls' varsity coach, I can say with absolutely no inhibition that our girls lived "Fleece 'em." They played with intensity and sportswomanship; they played with effort, enthusiasm and they were a classy group of young ladies—every one. I was proud of what they learned and I think they were proud of what I learned—or rather what they taught me—too!

Presently, I no longer coach at the varsity levels of either sport but do coach freshmen baseball and junior high basketball—for both girls and boys. I still try to instill in my young charges the lesson that I learned so long ago from a coaches' coach: Play the game—whatever the game may be—with intensity and gusto; give it everything you've got; leave everything on the court or field; play within the rules with respect for all participants; and be able to hold your head up knowing that you played the game the way it was meant to be played.

If you can look at yourself in the mirror and be happy with the person you see there, then you are a ferocious lady or ferocious gentleman, and you've achieved something special.

What is Class?

Class never runs scared. It is sure-footed and
confident in the knowledge that you can meet life
head on and handle whatever comes along.
Class never makes excuses. It takes its
lumps and learns from past mistakes.
Class is considerate of others.
It knows that good manners are nothing
more than a series of petty sacrifices.
Class bespeaks an aristocracy that has nothing to do
with ancestors or money. The most affluent blueblood
can be totally without class while the descendant of
a Welsh miner may ooze class from every pore.
Class never tries to build itself up by tearing others
down. Class is already up and need not strive to
look better by making others look worse.
Class can walk with kings and keep its virtue, and
talk with the crowds and keep the common touch.
Everyone is comfortable with the person who has
class because he is comfortable with himself.
If you have class you don't need much of anything
else. If you don't have class, no matter what else
you have doesn't make much difference.

—*Author Unknown*

Games Won or Lost Are Soon Forgotten . . . On Leaving a Legacy

Earlier in this book, you ran across a statement written by me:

"Games won or lost are soon forgotten, but the kind of person/team you are never will be."

This statement has been at the core of my coaching philosophy for many years. I can't recall for sure the circumstances when I first came up with it or even the first time I shared it with my players. I do know that it was very early in my career which began in the early '70's and it has been shared with every team I have coached since.

People's memories are about moments in time, not chunks of time. Memories are colored by our emotions that are the strongest felt during an experience and cause that experience to be indelibly etched into our psyches. I remember reading a quote somewhere that said, "Students may not remember what you taught them, but they will remember how you made them feel." What a tremendous reminder this has been for me!

And that is what I try to get my charges to understand about their participation in athletics. They are going to remember their teammates and how they felt about them much longer than they are going to recall what their won-lost record was in a particular season. At the very least, the memories of their teammates will be much more significant to them than the memory of the outcome of their games with the passage of time.

Trophies may get dusty and become items of clutter, but vivid memories of past glories shared with people who have become significant to you never lose their luster or prominence in our minds. Indeed, they—our memories—may be the most cherished of our possessions.

Part of the "games won or lost" philosophy that has been incorporated since I first used it is the challenge to my players (and students in the classroom as well) to leave a legacy—something positive and of significance—to those who follow them. A legacy is an inheritance in one way—something worth having and cherished by the recipient—as well as a torch that is passed as a responsibility for the recipient to bear, add to and bequeath to those who follow. Great organizations or programs with great traditions year in and year out have been able to inculcate this concept of leaving a legacy into their membership.

Another part of the philosophy is the "no regrets" part. I remind my students and athletes that their time in school or in season is finite—it will come to an end and they will never have this exact situation with these very same classmates or teammates again. Sure, they will probably be in other classes or on other teams, and maybe some of the same people will be there, but it will not be exactly like this one at this time. That is why each team or class should be special to them.

I try to have them look beyond the end of the year/season and then look back on the time they are spending doing what they are doing. I tell them that if I had a nickel for every student or athlete I've had over the years who told me they "wish they woulda tried harder, paid more attention, listened more, got better grades, done things differently . . ." I could have retired a few years ago! The point is, I am trying to get them to—as much as possible—live their lives with no regrets or second-guessing.

I want them to be as focused as possible on a mission of their choosing that is worth the effort and time of their lives that they are spending to achieve it. "Try as much as possible to be a person of no regrets," I tell them. "Though we are not perfect and we will make mistakes that we will regret along the way, at least don't let them be errors of omission rather than commission. Being at the end of your life with a bag of 'I wish I wouldas . . . ' signifies a wasted life. Make memories. Make something of yourselves. Aspire to live a life of no regrets."

Time is a precious gift not to be wasted. I close this chapter and this book with the piece, "This is a New Day," which was given to me by a dear friend, now deceased—my father-in-law—not long after I married his daughter. It captures the essence of all the components of my "games won or lost" philosophy and is one of the handouts that I share with all my students and athletes. My hope is that it will become as meaningful to them—and to you—as it has been to me.

A New Day

This is a new day.
I have this day to use as I will.
I can waste it
or use it for good.
What I do today is important
because I am exchanging
a day of my life for it.
When tomorrow comes,
this day will be gone forever,
leaving something in its place
that I have traded for it.
I want it
to be gain,
not loss–
good,
not evil–
success,
not failure.
I shall not forget the price I paid for it.

—*Author Unknown*

Endnotes

1. Granted swimming and golf are different individual sports because, in those sports, you are competing more against a clock or a course than you are going head to head against another individual. Nevertheless, the similarity is valid because the focus is on the individual's expertise and achievement when under the scrutiny of fans who, because of their presence, add pressure to performance.

2. Some may question the use of the word orderliness when describing the world because of the obvious turmoil that exists. I choose to use it because of my belief in the Biblical passage, "And we know that all things work together for good to them that love God." - Romans 8:28

3. Without getting too philosophical here, "self-love," from my perspective, is loving that part of myself that is comprised of the Spirit of my Creator, which, therefore, would make up a relationship between my Creator and myself.

4. First base is the only base that a runner may overrun without being tagged out, unless they make a deliberate move or step toward second base after he has crossed the base. Contrary to

popular belief, it does not matter which way a runner turns to go back to first base—out or in—as long as he does not take a step in the direction of second base. If there is no intent to advance past first base on the play, the runner may turn either way.

5. I am using the word "responding" here rather than reacting because of the intended depth of meaning in this situation. React means having sort of a knee jerk, push-push back, cause–effect approach, whereas the word respond implies a thoughtful answer to the situation at hand. We may react to certain stimuli, which is natural in some situations, but a response requires thoughtful recognition and interpretation of the situation and an answer that is more appropriate than perhaps a push-push back reaction.

6. Strategy plays an important role with a runner on third. Most teams will play fairly conservative with a runner on third and no outs. A ground ball, for example, must get through the infield before the runner is sent home or a fly ball must be hit very deep before the runner is sent. In other words, with no outs, the runner must be absolutely certain he can score before he heads toward the plate. Strategy may change with one out, with many teams taking a chance to score on contact on a ground ball, or tagging and trying to score on a fly ball that isn't hit too deeply. Many factors will be considered such as score, inning, pitcher, hitter, etc. when determining strategy in this situation.

Pete Doumit is available for baseball clinics or to be a speaker for clinics, organizations, workshops, seminars, conferences or conventions. He has presentations of varying lengths for team-building, leadership and motivation.

For additional information about having him as a speaker or presenter you can contact him at:

Pete Doumit
5232 Ridgeview Drive
Moses Lake, WA 98837

Phone: (509) 765–0599
e-mail: pdoumit6@yahoo.com